John Seymour Wood

Yale Yarns

Sketches of life at Yale University

John Seymour Wood

Yale Yarns
Sketches of life at Yale University

ISBN/EAN: 9783337035938

Printed in Europe, USA, Canada, Australia, Japan

Cover: Foto ©ninafisch / pixelio.de

More available books at **www.hansebooks.com**

YALE YARNS

SKETCHES OF LIFE AT YALE UNIVERSITY

BY

JOHN SEYMOUR

AUTHOR OF "GRAMERCY PARK," "A̶..."

"A college joke to cure the d..."

ILLUSTRATED

G. P. PUTNAM'S SONS
NEW YORK   LONDON
27 WEST TWENTY-THIRD STREET   24 BEDFORD STREET, STRAND
The Knickerbocker Press
1895

TO

HENRY E. HOWLAND

YALE '54

PREFACE.

THE difficulty of suiting every one in a college story is greater than the casual reader may imagine. Aside from the cheek of the young maiden which may not be incarnadined under any consideration, and the maiden aunt who sees an utter lack of refinement in the daily student life, there is the old grad. who says it is n't as it was in *his* day, and the undergrad. who maintains it is n't as it is in *his!* If you describe the life of the "rowdy element," you may offend the "digs"; if you confine yourself to the "better element"— the good boys—the "earnest workers," the smart young Junior asks if you are describing life in a State Normal school or a female reformatory; if you poke fun at the faculty you have a fine array of parents and guardians about your ears; if you tell of things that happened in your day, the *Courant* and witty little *Record* show you up for an absurd old fossil who ought to have sense enough to stay buried and not insist on coming to life again; if you are flippant or hint of the seamy side of college life, the ponderous old *Lit* may pronounce your effort worthless and condemn you as the "enemy of Yale,"—and if so, it would be better a thousand millstones were hanged about your neck at once, for the oldest and at the same time, the "youngest" magazine in America pronounces literary judgments which are terribly and wondrously final.

Then there arises the difficulty of slang. What slang shall your college hero use? Yesterday's, to-day's, or to-morrow's? Much of the slang of four years ago is dead now. Are your stories up to date? If so to-day, they will not be next year. The privilege of quoting from a recent letter of an undergrad. has been afforded us. It is *apropos* on this point. He says:

"To begin with, there are nearly four varieties of slang used in the University,—approximately one for each class. Very evident is this when you are in conversation with a Freshman, or what is better, have the good luck to overhear two of these infants discoursing on college life. They import, every year, the very latest Bowery style, and while most of it soon wears

Preface. vii

off, yet ear-marks remain, and if they strike the popular fancy, the phrase or word is handed down from class to class. There is no authentic 'cuss-word' as the boys say. We suit the word to the action at Yale. In society we use lamb-like expressions which would hardly be recognized on the field or in the Gym. The phrase, 'Cuss a little, it may help you,' is not by any means discountenanced. In such cases we have our private 'cuss-words,' which vary from the Dwight Hall heeler's 'goodness!' down to,—well, as far down as they go. In a community as large as this, there are always a few who at times find themselves in such peculiar positions, that even St. Peter himself would hardly know what to do without giving way a little. Not since Freshman year have I heard any low profanity, and that was by an intoxicated person."

So, kind, indulgent reader, let us offer our Yale Yarns as of a date somewhere in the '90's, and the slang that occurs in them of no particular date at all. Many of the sketches are founded on fact, but whether fact or fancy, if they serve to amuse, it is perhaps all that the writer, an old grad. himself, can ask. It will be seen that very little is said of the athletic side of college life,—this side is well known, perhaps too much so, in our daily press. One might easily imagine from the newspapers, athletics to be the sole occupation of students. In reality, as things are now constituted, only the few actively engage in the chief athletic contests. The vast array of "rooters," "heelers," "backers," etc., employ themselves while in college in serious and studious pursuits, and give vent to their enthusiasm only at stated intervals. It is the object of this series of light college sketches, of which the first volume, Mr. Post's *Harvard Stories*, has already become well known, to present pen pictures of life in our great universities, without bearing too heavily on any one particular class or set. Life at Yale is too complex to afford opportunities in a few stories of giving more than a brief account of incidental phases. We cannot purvey such a complete view as *Tom Brown at Oxford*, or *The Adventures of Verdant Green*, nor have we attempted to carry any one set of men through the four years, as in *College Days, or Harry's Career at Yale*,—we have simply gathered together and written out yarns which have been more or less known for a long time, and have never had a friend to give them lasting form. As such, O kind, indulgent reader, we relinquish them to you, hoping that you will enjoy reading them as much as we have putting them together.

J. S. W.

CONTENTS.

	PAGE.
PREFACE	v
ONE ON THE GOVERNOR	1
THE OLD FENCE	20
IN THE POLITICAL CAULDRON	42
"LITTLE JACK" HORNER'S PIE	59
WITH THE DWIGHT HALL HEELERS	75
THE "DWARF'S" PROM.	94
THE LAST CRUISE OF THE "NANCY BRIG"	121
OLD SLEUTH'S LEVEL HEAD	139
NAT HALE, OF '73	156
THE DAWN TEA	175
THE GREAT SPRINGFIELD GAME	197
IN THE TOILS OF THE ENEMY	208
AN HYPNOTIC SEANCE	230
A VIOLENT REMEDY	247
"CHUMS OVER IN OLD SOUTH"	272
COMMENCEMENT	294

ILLUSTRATIONS.

	PAGE
VANDERBILT HALL	*Frontispiece.*
THE GYMNASIUM	24
OSBORN HALL	50
THE ART BUILDING	86
WELCH HALL	128
LAWRANCE HALL	178

YALE YARNS.

ONE ON THE GOVERNOR.

THEY were sitting in Sprague and Paige's room in Durfee, after supper, in the first week in October, smoking.

It was the very agreeable and comfortable twilight hour when even the "greasy grinds" hardly felt it in their hearts to begin the evening's cram. The crowd that made the air blue in the room were anything but "greasy grinds." A big wiry fellow in a white sweater was lounging half out of the window, talking and laughing with some men on the sidewalk below. Inside the room you could cut the smoke with a commons knife. Outside, the fading twilight made more beautiful and cathedral-like the long vista of old elms behind North College.

The evening was warm and windows were open, and festive sounds of the banjo floated out, and there came a tenor note far away from Farnam, which, if not calculated to soothe a soul in purgatory, was at least the cause of some sophomore profanity and a loud command to the tenor to go to a "worser place."

"Dwarf" Sprague, the big fellow in the sweater, called down out of the window:

"Jack, come up and give us that horse on Tom Keith's,—your chum's governor."

The man in the window called down again and the voice replied from below:

"What horse?"

"Oh, you know,—about the barn he fired——"

"What barn?"

"Say, Jack, you rascal, come up and get a good licking anyway,—and tell us the story."

"Dwarf" Sprague, the big fellow, pulled himself inside the room from the window, saying: "'Little Jack' Horner is out here. Make him come up and tell that horse on his chum's dad last summer."

Two or three fellows lounged to the window and looked down, hands in pockets.

"Come up, Jack Horner," said one, whose name, by the way, is William. "Come up, thou son of a grad, and if thou hast a horse on thy dad, or thy chum's dad, then tell it!"

"What was the story?" asked another.

"That's what we're trying to find out!" laughed a third.

"Wait! I'll go down and rush him up, and hold him till he tells it!" said the "Dwarf."

There was a silence when the "Dwarf" ran out of the room, speedily interrupted by one at the window crying:

"Dick Sprague has caught him,—got him by the collar and scruff of the neck,—and, by Jove! is running him in and up the stairs two steps at a time!"

Immediately after the door burst open, and——

"Hullo Bill—hullo Tom—hullo Paige—Nelson, is that you?" came from "Little Jack" Horner's panting lips, as Sprague, laughing, conducted him into the room. "I say, drop it, 'Dwarf'! Can't you get over your Freshman foolishness? I never came up-stairs so easily though in my life! I felt as light as I did in the boat two years ago. Light up here, some of you, and let's see how many chumps are hidden away here in the dark! 'All silent and all damned.'—Tell me, is all the class packed in behind the sofa? Get up, 'Lazy' Aldrich and shake. I can see *you*, Adolphus Austin!"

When the gas was lit, the funniest, fattest, smallest, roundest, queerest little man in college, appeared breast high to the study table, topped by a Y. U. B. C. cap on his round little head.

"Little Jack" Horner had the honor of steering Yale 'Varsity in great shape through a lane of yachts and booming cannon two years before, because of which, much was thereafter forgiven him. The little chap in his Freshman year was but a dot on the landscape, and weighed but eighty pounds. The crew of that year tossed him about on rainy days instead of a dumb bell! But once they broke training "Little Jack" Horner, they say, actually followed the career of his namesake. He did nothing ever after but

> Sat in a corner
> Eating his Xmas pie.

"He ate more pies, besides," said Paige,

"everything, in fact, he could lay his hands on. He went off yachting, and they said he'd disappear for hours and they'd find him hiding behind a cracker barrel, munching away, with a broad grin on his face, and no one knows how much truck and crackers in his little 'tum.'" But it may be concluded that Paige was envious.

"He came back to college after the race," continued Paige, "and ate away on the sly, ordering himself, say, a great dinner at the New Haven House, and then slipping off to Traeger's and pretending he had n't dined, and putting down a fresh brace of chops and beer. When Captain Sprague, of the crew, caught him at it one day and admonished him, he said:

"'See here, Cap., all last year while you fellows ate all the beef and turkey you could,— and dined off the very best at the training-table,—you were starving me! You could see through me,—I had a pane in my stomach nearly all the time, and you tried to make me a small edition of the living skeleton. You go find some other fool of a Freshman coxwain! I've coxed my last crew. You hear *me!* Why, last year every time I looked at a potato, you gave me a piece—of your lip! And as for a pie or a pudding, or any grub fit to eat,— Lord Harry!—So, old man, no more races for me—Thanks!'"

And they could not persuade him.

At the present time "Little Jack" Horner was not in training, ate and drank what he liked, and he certainly liked a good deal, and rarely was seen without a large, gold-tipped "Egyptian Deity" in his mouth. He edged himself up on the table, after a little chaffing, and told this tale of a grad.:

"You know my chum,—Tom Keith? Well, this horse is on his awful dad.

"My chum's father is a judge out in Michigan. He is an old grad., and a solemn, pompous, dignified old grad. at that. When my chum was jugged and rusticated last June, just before Commencement, he came on here, and there was, I deeply regret, the devil to pay.

"You know Tom had n't done anything very much,—only absorbed a little weak Soph. punch, and had to go off and paint tutor Blink's door red, and the town afterwards, and crook signs, and all that. I was with him, but *he* got caught, and I did n't. Poor chap! Well, when Hon. Elias J. Keith, of the Supreme Court, Michigan, came on here to fix it up with the Faculty, score my chum, and incidentally attend his class reunion,— there was trouble enough over at 1279, Lawrance, and I hung crape on the door. How he did bullyrag my poor, beloved chum! one of the dearest, gentlest chaps in the world, you know. Jerusalem! he jawed right and left and up and down for four mortal hours, and then passed sentence. Tom should be cut down half his allowance the rest of his college course. Tom should not go abroad with the rest of the family last summer. Tom should be made to do this and to do that,—and the name of Keith was tarnished forever,—and,—well, poor Tom looked plowed enough to go and jump off long wharf at the end of the lecture. When he stopped for want of breath, I asked the old man, as cool as I could: ' Judge Keith,—you were at Yale, were you not?'

" ' I was, sir, in the class of 'umpty-eight——'

" And you never,—er—got caught in any scrape, I suppose, while you were at Yale?"

" He gave me a queer look, then said, angrily:

"'Scrape? I? No, sir, and let me tell you, sir——'

"One moment,—I never have myself, but—I may say, perhaps you and I are more fortunate—so you, too, *were never caught?*

"By Jove, he looked daggers at me, but he said not a word; put on his hat and left the room. Tom looked like a faded ghost, and said he never saw his governor so wholesale mad in all his life before. He wished I had kept quiet.

"Well,—so Tom packed his trunk and went off to rusticate at New London—he did n't mind *that!*—and I hung around over Commencement, just wondering how I could get even with his awful dad in some way.

"I hung around like an old Gaboriau detective, and waited,—and I kept my eye on Judge Keith. He waited, too, over till the next week, when his class was to have its Quinquagentennial reunion dinner,—old grads. are always dining or being dined,—or something of that sort, at Commencement, and they were to have Judge Keith preside, and it was to be a grand affair, at three dollars a head, at the New Haven House.

"Well, a lot of those 'umpty-eight men came back to college. Regular old fossils some of 'em,—talked about loss of the fence,—talked about the loss of the old State House on the green,—seemed to feel the Faculty were accountable for that too! I got in with some of them. I drank with 'em, treated 'em, called myself a ''umpty eater' too; and, by Jove! those old cocks are right down good smooth fellows, too, do you know it? I got all the information I possibly could about Judge Elias B. Keith, of Michigan. Gad! he stood fourth in his class, he was a sort of model,—took a philosophical, —was a regular plug in college,—and there did n't seem to be a flaw in him, and I was about giving up in disgust and going down to New London to see how the crew were doing, when an 'umpty-eighter, by the name of—of—I forget his name—a Philadelphia lawyer—but he was a hummer, and put down in one evening, to my actual count, five whiskey cocktails, six beers, three Manhattans, and a bottle of fizz at Traegers,—we matched for this, and he got stuck. I asked *him* about the Judge, and, by George, I struck it rich! If he had n't been somewhat jagged, he never would have given it away;—*in vino veritas*, you know. But he told a heavy one on Elias B.!

"I said (call him Jones)—I said, Mr. Jones, you get Judge Keith to tell that joke at your dinner, will you? When things get mellow you know, and you all get reminiscencing. Get him to confess it——"

"Gad, I will though,—it's so long since,—only three of us know it. I'll get his old chum now Rev. Dr. Bailey to ask him. Yes, it will be a good joke,—we'll make him confess it—after all these years! And we'll have a laugh on him——"

"Oh, it will be excellent, Mr. Jones! And I made him shake on it and promise he'd do it, and by Jove, old Jones, was as good as his word, too, and so, 'he done it!'"

"Little Jack" Horner slapped his fat little thigh, and rolled to and fro on the table, convulsed with laughter at anticipation, as he spoke.

"The next night—the night of the dinner—came. There were just forty-four old 'umpty-eighters present, still able and willin' to carry a fork to their chins. I had not been idle that day myself, as you will soon perceive; but that is neither here nor there, as they often say of a lost sparkler.

"The night of the dinner came. Fellows, they were as smooth a looking set of old men as you ever saw; and Judge Keith sat at the head of the long table, proud as,—proud as I was once in New London. Some had bald heads; some had too much hair; some had whiskers, some had none; all were a good sturdy lot of Yale grads. as you ever saw. I stood in the doorway and looked 'em over. After they had all got seated, in strolled a long, lanky, dusty hayseed Westerner, about seven feet high, in a slouch hat and a linen duster, umbrella, and carpet bag. No one knew him, and he marched right in though, and just called out: 'Is this the class of 'umpty-eight?' They said 'Yes,' and he sat down at the table without a word. A murmur of surprise went around the room, and a man at the other end of the room shouted '*Perkins?*' and the lank Westerner said, '*Right!*'—dropped in Freshman year for stealing the chapel Bible and exchanging it with Harvard.' Then those fellows gave a cheer, for Perkins is an M.C. now, you know, and they had n't seen him for years—and the way Perkins set up fizz along the table, was a caution."

"We had beaten Harvard that afternoon at the Field, you know, and they all felt *they* had done it, and they were happy as kings, and so I let 'em feed and went off and packed my trunk to get away the next day for the races, and again strolled in the room where they sat about ten o'clock. The speeches had just begun as I came in, and *such* speeches! Eloquence cut no ice at *that* dinner! It was just fun and give and take, and they got off old jokes and sang 'Neath the Elms' and 'Bingo,' 'Here's to Good Old Yale,' and those old-timers. And at last up gets the Rev. Dr. Bailey and tells about the Judge,—what a great man he was, and how he had risen to be one of the greatest lawyers in the West, and all that, and how they all knew it would be so when he was in college, and how immaculate and good he had been,— always, even in college—'I knew it, for I was his chum,' said Bailey, '*except on one occasion!*'

"By Jove! the room was so still you could hear a dumb-bell drop.

"'Give us that occasion,' roared my friend

Jones and others, as loud as they could roar,—
I roared too to keep up the excitement.

"I stood near the door and watched. Gad! they got the Judge up on his feet to tell them! I beat my sides with joy just then and could hardly contain myself.

"'I suppose my old chum refers,' said the Judge, laughing, 'to my attempt to steal a turkey, and in doing so set a barn afire?'

"To nearly all the 'umpty-eighters this came with a great shock. Gee! they broke out in howls of delight, and hammered the table with their spoons and glasses. When it was quiet again, Judge Keith said, as if very much tickled; 'I was very fortunate in that it was never found out that I did it. I went out after turkey,— out here, away off by West Rock. You can believe I never went near the spot afterwards. A farmer out there—I believe, if my memory serves me right, his name was Higgins—Higgins was famous in those days for his fat turkeys, and about Thanksgiving time—in my Junior year,—that was in the fall of '67,—it was our custom then to forage about and capture one or two (laughter). I got into the barn where the turkeys were, and it was so dark I lit a match to see which one I should select. Well, the match snapped and broke and fell in a pile of hay. In a moment to my horror, it was ablaze! I dropped the turkey I had seized and ran like the wind to where my confederates were waiting for me in a buggy. 'Drive home quick some roundabout way!' I said, as I jumped in, 'I've set the barn afire!' It was a small shed—we would hardly call it a barn out in my country—no horses or cattle in it, and we drove off in a hurry. Pretty soon the flames could be seen a mile away over the trees. Well, I imagine Farmer Higgins had roast turkey that night, though it must have been pretty well crisped,' and the Judge sat down, laughing as if he would split.

"As the 'umpty-eighters applauded and laughed, an old man—older than any of them, even,—a horny-handed son of toil, with a long white beard, stepped out from a doorway and waited until every one became silent, then said, in a cold hard voice, turning to the Judge:

"'So you be the student feller what set afire to my turkey shed, be ye? I be Farmer Higgins, that's who I be.'

"The Judge,—he turned all colors, but said not a word. I shook in my shoes.

"The farmer turned to all the 'umpty-eighters, in midst of a dead silence.

"'I call on ye all to witness he confessed right here he burned Farmer Higgins's barn in 1867. Now, I allus sed I'd ketch the reskell student feller as done it,—an' now I hev.'

"The Judge rose, astonished, very much chagrined.

"'Oh, don't you say you did n't or try fer to get aout the State; if ye do I'll jest hev ye arrested, and put through; an' there's an officer outside as I ken call handy,—an' I've got my liar here too.'

"At these words, a rummy-looking old pettifogger, Old Bum Busby, who hangs about the City Hall and takes a police 'case' for a drink, stepped forward, and in a very solemn and impressive manner, and very husky voice, said, 'Gents, thish is a very serious case—State-prison offense—arson—first degree,—while committin' act of robbery, as I meself heerd defendant Keith confess.'

"'But it's over twenty years ago!' exclaimed

the Judge, perspiration pouring down his brow. 'It 's outlawed.'

"'Don't keer tuppence fer that. You 've been out the State sence. Jedge Keith, as bein' a liar yerself ye'd orter know, statoot don't run then. You 'll hev to do time fer it, sir. Arson, sir. Bad sort of scrape, sir. Would n't a thought it of you!'

"Several of the brash 'umpty-eighters rose up in a state bordering on consternation and wanted to throw the old farmer and his lawyer out of the window, but the Judge waived them back. Some laughed at the affair as a capital joke, others shook their heads and looked solemn.

"'At last my sin has found me out!' said the Judge, gravely, and by Jove, fellows, I felt awfully sorry then I had put up the grind on him. He was a sensitive, scrupulous sort of man, and he felt the disgrace keenly there before his class,—and they 'd just been trying to guy him on account of his having a son suspended.

"Then up rose my friend Jones. 'I begin to smell a mice,' he laughed. 'It was I who told this story to a fat little chap—now in college,—

Horner, by name; it's all *his* doing, I believe.'

"'My son's chum,' said the Judge, 'William Horner!'

"'And he has probably done this for a joke. Come now, 'Lias, did not you scold your boy pretty well on his being disciplined? I understand so. This is the way his friend retaliates!'

"Just about then things were getting rather hot and mixed and, I was not wanting to have my hair pulled particularly by those 'umpty-eighters, so I slid out and ran home to my room in Lawrance and bolted the door.

"You see, I'd fixed it with the farmer to divvy up on what he got out of the Judge in 'settlement,' would you believe it—the farmer got $200!—and later, that night, I sneaked out and met him at the pettifogger Busby's office, and the honest old chap acted on the square, chuckled at the joke, and gave me a hundred, and we all went out and had a 'bot.' I gave the lawyer twenty-five dollars, which paid him for his trouble and for his services a year ago, too, getting me out of the jug—you remember the time—without the Faculty knowing it, and I carried the balance up to New

London next day and doubled it on the race. I gave the hundred and fifty to my chum at New London, and told him to put it on a horse that my old friend, the pettifogger Busby, told me over his cups was sure to win the Brooklyn handicap that day following. By Jupiter! it did! and Keith wrote his dad next day—his dad had gone home—a sanctimonious letter, enclosed a draft for two hundred dollars, what *he* had paid Farmer Higgins, explaining that he had earned it by tutoring and he felt that it was but right to pay it, and we had over three hundred dollars left, which we used up in Boston, with some jolly, smooth Harvard Willies, Jack Rattleton, Holworthy, Stoughton & Company, in just a week's time!'

When "Little Jack" Horner finished, some one said, laughing:

"A good hoss on the old grad.!"

"But that is n't all, *quite*," chuckled the little fat sinner. "The Judge sent the draft back, and wrote an abject letter of apology for giving Tom such a raking down, when it was only 'boy's foolishness,' and said if he 'd not mention *his* affair at home, *he* would n't mention Tom's suspension, and that it was just as well he *was* rusticated a part of the ensuing fall, as he would have a longer period of travel abroad, and they 'd try to get back in time to see the game at Springfield. So my chum came out all right, you see, and we put that extra two hundred dollars in at Newport and the Pier. Tom Keith had just seventy-five cents in his pocket when he met his family on the *Teutonic*, July 15th, and sailed for Liverpool."

"Little Jack" had such a smirk of comfortable satisfaction on his fat little face over his getting even with the old grad., that "Dwarf" Sprague could not resist laying him over his knee (Sprague was on Little Jack's famous crew and always felt like a father to him). "You fat little tell-tale!" he cried, whacking him. "I'll teach you to get old grads. into trouble!"

THE OLD FENCE.

Up to the time when the march of improvement began, which has ended with the beautiful Vanderbilt Hall and the complete enclosure of the campus, the fence, from the path near the corner on College Street around the corner of Chapel and up to South College, was the one great institution of Yale. Tradition fades quickly in college, and the student of to-day is inclined to smile at the expression of regret for the fence's loss to which the old grad. is apt to give vent on returning to New Haven.

There is no loafing-place now for the poor old alumnus, and he is apt to wander about staring vaguely at the new buildings and feeling that Yale has gone ahead in a most startling and sensational manner the last ten years, and left him behind a forlorn and melancholy relic of the past.

Yet he is glad, too, to see Yale's material progress. He is always delighted to read of the latest princely benefaction; like Artemus Ward his relatives in the war, he is ever willing to sacrifice his brother alumni, if they will only leave in their wills a few hundred thousand to Yale. It mitigates the sadness of a classmate's death to read that his Alma Mater is often the gainer by it. Dear old Bob Jones was the best fellow that ever lived—many a rarebit and mug of Bass have we had with him at the "Quiet House," tidily kept by one Mrs. Moriarty; many a good time we've had together at Rood's, at Gus Traeger's, at Charley Bradley's, but we observed that in his will one hundred and fifty thousand dollars goes to Yale on the death of his son Robert, Jr., and we fall to wondering (and hoping?) whether Robert, Jr., is a sickly young man?

The dear old fence!

On it men crammed for recitation; read the newspapers; interchanged stories; gossiped; talked athletics; got acquainted; sung songs; flirted with passing girls; lived. The fence over in front of Durfee is something like it in a feeble sort of way, but it's not quite the same thing. There was always some wandering musician who played, or a boot-black who shone for five cents, or an influx of grads. up from New York, or the passing of a pretty girl, to create a diversion on the old fence. It was the centre of the good-hearted, manly, democratic Yale, and when it was taken away there were many forebodings by the grads. as to the future character of Yale life. So far the prophecy of the encroachment of moneyed aristocracy is hardly borne out. The college still preserves the character of twenty years ago in its regard for a purely democratic standard of manliness and worth. The rich man's son has still to fight his own battles, and frequently to overcome a certain democratic prejudice against him. He succeeds, in spite of his income, and his friends like him only because he acts and carries himself like a man.

The Hon. W. D. Horner, of 'umpty-three—"Little Jack's" father came on for a few days last May, to see his son, and had a great deal to say about the absence of the fence. He growled a good deal at first over Osborne Hall—said the fence was worth a dozen of such ornate examples of Rococo and the Renaissance. He had n't been back since his class reunion in '83. He growled a good deal about the death of

Linonia and Brothers, too, but that was too much out of date for rhyme or reason, and they laughed at him.

They got the old grad. to telling some old fence reminiscences one night at Mory's (he declared Mory's was n't like the old "Quiet House" on Court Street in the faintest degree). Among them were the following yarns which were gathered and written out by Paige afterwards:

" In my day no peeler was allowed inside the yard, and to-day I saw one hanging about—on the old chapel steps! I don't like *that!* Many's the time we used to be chased by peelers until we got to the campus, then we jumped the fence and defied them to come on. They did n't dare, in my day, to go inside.

" Freshmen were n't allowed on the fence until they reached third term, but the biggest fight I ever saw arose out of our class seizing, in winter term, Fresh. year, the fence and holding it. Freshmen sat on the College Street side only. If they tried to sit on the Soph. fence, they were rolled in the mud, and promptly punished for their presumption.

" Oh, there **are** lots of queer things which

happened on and about the fence. I wish I could recall more of them. One night about twenty New Haven girls dressed up as men took possession of the Junior fence. They carried canes, wore high hats, and tried to smoke cigarettes. The boys found them out and then there was fun! The whole college got out after a while and built them a bonfire, and escorted them home.

"Then, at the fence, the Glee Club used to make its first public appearance at night. The New Haven House windows were crowded with people. A bouquet or even a flower thrown out of a window was grabbed for by the students with the avidity street arabs grab for pennies. Sometimes they'd throw cabbages!

"I remember when the Freshmen of 'umpty-two, enraged at not being allowed the fence, tore the whole thing down and carried it off up Prospect Street one rainy night, and in the morning there wasn't a trace of it, not even gate-posts! The Faculty made them rebuild it at their own expense. It was set afire hundreds of times. 'Umpty-nine's boys had a canvas canopy built over it in their Junior year, for

THE GYMNASIUM.

rainy days, but the Faculty made them take it down.

"In 1870, I think it was, the Sophs. ran an electric wire along the Freshman fence and gave them a tremendous shock one evening. The Freshmen got even by sawing the Soph. fence so that it went down with them when they were roosting on it.

"I never shall forget the scare the Sophs. put up one evening on the whole college. It was a warm June evening and every one was out on the fence after supper, smoking, singing, and enjoying the air. Suddenly we heard the awful cry of 'Mad dog! Mad dog' coming up from down Chapel, and a big lean hound, foaming at the mouth, came tearing along up the street. You ought to have seen that fence scatter! Some ran as far as North College. The dog kept right on up Chapel and disappeared up York, evidently having business of it's own somewhere in the suburbs. Tied to its tail was a white flag with the Soph. numeral on it. They'd made the dog chew soap like a tragedy actor. There was a great laugh all over college over that mad dog. The Sophs. set up a couple of kegs of beer on it and were forgiven.

"The only distinct romance I ever heard about the fence was told me by Suydam, of '59—a true story.

"There was a daughter of a New Haven gentleman (who is dead now), who was a very beautiful girl. She was the toast of the college in those days, and all the students were wild over her—especially the Southerners, who were numerous in those days before the war. I've forgotten her name now, but will call her Marion Brown for want of a better.

"She used to drive, herself, a pair of lively black horses in a phaeton, and you may believe she very often turned the corner of Chapel and College, and gave many a smile and a bow to her friends among the students, who were seated on the fence.

"One day as she drove past the colleges, a contemptible Freshman let off a huge cannon-cracker under her carriage; the horses took fright, and Marion, not wishing to run away down College or Chapel, pulled them squarely into the fence. Jim Thompson was sitting there and made a dash for the horses' bits, but was carried under and trampled on. Marion was thrown out and they picked her up without a scratch. Thompson was badly hurt and had a leg broken. Well, she insisted on his being taken home to her father's house, where she nursed him, and now they're married and have a son in Sheff."

Mr. Horner lit a fresh cigar — and continued:

"There was a time during a revival, along in the early '70's, when the class deacons made the fence the centre of a noonday open-air prayer-meeting. This was finally broken up by a few wicked Sophs. who exploded cannon-crackers and hired a brass band to play waltzes at the same time, and the deacons had to retire, discomfited.

"Oh, the fence was always the centre of things in the old times, from religion to the worship of Bacchus. Along about twelve and one o'clock at night and later, many a night have parties of students, after a wine supper at Bradley's, or an ale party at Mory's, or a 'beer or two' at Gus Traeger's, made the night hideous at the fence, with songs and skylarking. They used to have tight-rope performances on it, and set it on fire, and paint it with tar and red paint, and do pretty much everything they could to it—and students always were pretty versatile in such matters.

"I remember a story of a tramp when Professor S—— was in college. He and several classmates had been down to Mory's, and when they got back to the fence, about twelve one night, they fell in with an old tramp sitting there, and had some fun with him. They couldn't get the old hobo to leave and go off to bed. He just sat there and wouldn't budge. They pulled him off several times, but it didn't do any good. He said 'he wanted to hear de birds sing in the morning, and see de sun rise, and he was just going to sit dere and smoke a pipe and wait fer de morning.'

"Finally, they all went off and left him alone, sitting there 'just thinking,' he said, 'and waiting for de morn to come.' Then one of the students, on getting to his room, found a cannon cracker and they thought they'd go and let it off just underneath the old hobo, and see if he wouldn't move on.

"So they got the fire cracker, and stole up noiselessly where he was sitting and lit the fuse, and stole away and hid behind the elms and waited for results.

The Old Fence.

"The old tramp sat with his head bowed on his hands, motionless, in just the same attitude in which they had left him, 'waiting fer de morn.'

"Well, the cannon cracker went off like blazes and made a devil of a noise and shook the whole college like an earthquake (it was one o'clock in the morning), and many a pale and frightened tutor leaped from his bed, and rushed to the window in the old brick row to see what was up.

"But the old tramp just sat there, pipe in mouth, and did n't move. The cracker nearly set his ragged coat-tails on fire, but he did n't seem to notice it at all.

"They went up stealthily and shouted in his ear. He did n't turn his head. They shook him and then drew back, horrified and aghast. The old tramp was dead!

"They felt of him,—he was cold; and they felt relieved to find his sudden taking off was not due to their nonsense; and then, scared at what had happened, they ran off to their rooms, leaving him there on the Senior fence, dead, still sitting and waiting for the morn to come."

There was a silence as the old grad. finished

this last yarn, and then "Little Jack" said, in his inimitable way: "And what did the Faculty say in the morning?"

"My son, they decided the old tramp was fitted to enter the medical school, and up there on York Street they gave him a *post-mortem* examination! *I understand he passed it successfully!*"

After the smiles at his gruesome jest had subsided, Mr. Horner told this further little yarn of the old fence:

"In those days when I was in college, the crew used to train very differently from the way they do now. The work was much more severe. The diet was principally raw beef. They drank only a half pint of water a day, at noon; no ale or beer, and kept at work almost all their waking hours. One of the first things, when they arose at five o'clock in the morning, was to run at top speed fifty times up and down their entries, from top to bottom, 'to get their hearts working.' It made brutes of those it did n't kill. They trained as if for a prize fight, running sometimes twelve or eighteen miles a day, and rowing as much again.

"Well, Hardwell was captain one year, and

he was a wiry old soldier, without any soft spot about him. He was about thirty years old, and had been a scout on the plains until he struck it rich in a Colorado mine and came on East to be educated. He was a terror, and with all his rigor and vigor, he ruined his crew by overwork, and Harvard beat us that year by over a minute.

"There was one thing he did believe in — whiskey, and the crew got all of that they needed, and, of course, it was not the best thing for them,—raw whiskey. It made them all look like thin red crows most of the time. Raw meat and whiskey would spoil any crew, and yet old Captain Hardwell had the entire confidence of the college. They knew—we all knew—he was faithful and hardworking and anxious to win, and so mad when licked the summer previous that he offered to take a bowie knife and go alone over to Harvard's quarters on Lake Quinsigamond, and 'ventilate' their stomachs one by one, in the most blood-curdling Western style! He was a sort of college hero in his day and generation, and he knew less about rowing than I do about algebra. He knew a great deal about discipline, and mortifying the flesh, and hard work and little sleep, and making everybody who differed with him feel the weight of his fist too.

"Well, the fierce old martinet was sitting on the fence one night, and some busybody came and told him that two of the crew were out walking with a couple of shop girls, and old Hardwell swore a mighty oath.

"'What the blankety blank do they want to go and soften 'emselves up with girls for, and the race only three weeks off!'

"Then he got down off the fence and strode off to his room, and they knew something was in the wind,—something alarming.

"The next morning, those going to breakfast early saw a sight. Captain Hardwell tarred and feathered and tied to the Soph. fence, where he'd been nearly all night!

"When released, he said nothing, but went straight to his room, got off what tar he could, packed his grip and got out of New Haven by the first train and never showed up there again. No, never has been here since, either.

"It seems he went to his room on hearing about the members of the crew flirting with shop girls, and got down his heavy army revolver, loaded it and started out for bear. He hunted the men and their girls down, and it turned out they were n't shop girls at all, but sisters of one of the men. They were walking and chatting in York Square when the Captain 'caught' them. And then and there he gave them a powerful tongue lashing, interspersed with certain cursory matter, which will naturally not bear repeating. Well, being before the two girls who were frightened nearly to death, the two crew men were driven to fury. The Captain made them leave the girls and go back to college and then go straight to bed. He literally drove them down the street, flourishing his revolver, and stood over them too until they ducked under their coverlids.

"Well, when the storm subsided and *he* went off to bed, the entire crew got up about midnight and went to his room, overpowered the old cuss, carried him bodily down to the fence, and lashed him to it so tight he couldn't move. Then they heated some tar and poured it all over him. You see, they got so sick of his tyranny they could n't endure it any longer. When Hardwell left, they elected another man captain, but it was too late in the season and Harvard beat us again that year, just the same.

"Oh, there are a lot more yarns about the fence," said the old grad., yawning, " but I've forgotten them. It was a great institution, in the old days.

" I remember once, before the new buildings had been put up to spoil the Campus, and before the days of peelers, and while the old stucco State House still stood in all its beautiful Grecian simplicity of outline on the green, a joke played on an old farmer, who evidently was from up the country somewhere and had no suspicions of the student capacity for playing pranks.

"You see, the old hayseed had imagined he had a perfect right to hitch his team to our fence, a sacrilege which, as soon as we got out of morning recitation, we Sophs. were not slow to marvel at, and punish.

" What dire fate should overtake that team of roan and piebald old farm horses, who had already dared to nibble the top round of our fence while their owner had gone off about his business? How should justice be meted out to that old farmer?

"We thought of many plans, to load the wagon with hay and set fire to it; to hitch the team in again backwards, and put the cart before the horse; or to paint one horse red and the other blue, but at last Jim Hayward, the poet of our class, and a man of the most brilliant imagination, hit on this scheme, which we carried out to the letter.

"We drove that piebald and roan team over near the State House and unhitched it.

"The building was not in use at the time, and a flight of broad stairs led up all the way to the very roof, which was nearly flat and covered with slate.

"Well, we led those old farm horses one by one up the stairs,—don't look surprised, horses will go up-stairs with great ease; it's just the opposite with horses as it was with the man in Virgil who found it so easy to *descend* to Avernus; you can't get a horse down-stairs very well, but it is a pleasant pastime to lead him up. Well, we led those horses one by one up and on the roof of the State House. Yes, sir; if you don't believe it, go get me a notary!

"Then we took that wagon apart and carried it all up, piece by piece, and set it up again on the roof and hitched the piebald and roan horse to it and tied them to a chimney; then we came down and lay low for the farmer when he should come back and get his team.

"I never saw anything so absurd in my life; there, up in the air, sixty feet or so above ground, on that flat slate roof, stood that old roan and piebald team, as natural as life, just as though they belonged up there, hitched to a chimney!

"People stopped and stared at the team, and rubbed their eyes to see if they were really awake and not dreaming! A great crowd began to gather. We lay down in the grass on the Campus, behind the elms—we *had* grass in those days,—and rolled about dead tired, but well pleased with the joke. We were laying for the hayseed farmer to come back and look for his team. I may say we were pretty tired, too, for it was hard work getting the farm wagon up there, and putting it together again, and it was a warm June day.

"Presently up he came from Chapel Street, —a horny-handed, long-bearded old fellow, with a slouch hat and long linen duster on, and his trousers tucked into his boot tops. He was

The Old Fence.   37

walking a little unsteadily as he came up, and we could see the neck of a black bottle protruding from one of the side pockets of his duster. Evidently the long time he had been absent, —some two hours,—was accounted for by his attendance at the shrine of Bacchus. He stared about vacantly a minute—'Say, boys, seen anythin' o' my team I tied ter the fence yere?' he asked.

"'What team?' said I.

"'Why, a piebald an' roan hoss, an' waggin. Tied right yere to this fence.'

"'Why, it seems to me I did see a team; piebald, you say?'

"'Yes, piebald and roan.'

"'Was it your team?'

"'Why, yes; come in fro' the farm with a load of potatys. Wonder if they got onhetched and wandered off somewheres?'

"'You say piebald and roan horse?'

"'Yes.'

"'I did see a team going off by themselves over to the State House.'

"'Why, that 's 'em; State Hus', ye say?'

"'Yes.'

"The farmer wandered over in that direction

himself, and we followed him to see the sport.

"By this time several hundred people had gathered, staring up at the team on the State House. Street gamins were shouting and jeering; old men were discussing it, astonished; ladies stopped in their carriages and wondered. The whole college came out to see the fun, and the farmer alone in all that crowd had not caught sight of his team.

"'Seen my team, folks?' he asked. 'Piebald and roan?'

"Then he glanced up at the State House, and may I die if I ever saw a human being so utterly knocked silly!

"There stood the team of old nags, half asleep, quietly tied to the chimney, as if it was the most proper place for them in the world! It seemed too positively absurd to be true!

"Well, the farmer just stared at his team for fully five minutes, in speechless and whimsical terror. Then he said:

"'I told Marier I would n't tech a drop, an' it 's a jest punishment ter me, that 's what 't is.'

"Then he asked an old man if *he* saw a team

up there on the State House roof, and the old man said: 'Yes, but if I 'd been drinking as you have, I 'd go and sign the pledge at once on seeing such a sight!'

"'Gosh all hemlock!' cried the farmer. 'Haow in thunder did they git up there?'

"Then he just sat down on the grass and stared. 'There they be,' he said, 'lookin' nat'ral as life thet there piebald 'n roan. Gosh all hemlock! But haow they come fer to wanter stan' on thet roof, I can't see. It beats me.'

"Then he took a long pull at his black bottle, and lay down in the grass, as if utterly overcome in mind and body.

"Then he sat up again. 'Yes, there they be!' he cried. 'Piebald and roan.—It ain't no mistake!'

"Then he started off after his team, and the next thing we saw, he 'd got up on the roof himself, with a number of small boys following him, and then we saw him lie down in the bottom of his wagon, and apparently go to sleep in a state of hopeless despair—and rum.

"We had to go into noon recitation then, and when we came out he was still there, and the whole city of New Haven had turned out to look at the sight. It was one of the greatest gags ever gotten off at Yale!"

"How did they get the team down?"

"Well, it took four days, and they had to hand-feed the horses all that time. Finally they got out the city fire department, and got the horses down the stairs backwards, and the farmer went home a wiser and better man. I remember we made up a purse for him, and he invited a lot of us out to his farm, over behind West Rock, to come out and drink hard cider but we never accepted his invitation.

"But it was a warning to all farmers and townies to let our sacred fence alone, and it was never defamed again that way, until it had to go to make room for Osborne Hall."

"Little Jack" (a chip of the old block) hummed quietly:

> "Wonder if it 's true,—
> Does it seem so to you?
> Seems to me he 's lyin'—
> Oh, I wonder if it 's true?"

Then, as it was late, they had one more round of Bass and Burton ale at Mory's, and strolled home, singing an old-time song, of a society long defunct:

The Old Fence.

"*Amici usque ad alteras.*"

"And not necessarily friends—*after* the altar," said the old grad., pleasantly, "for then boys, your wives usually select your friends for you!"

IN THE POLITICAL CAULDRON.

"HONEST John, the thief," had been brushing up the room (No. 874 Welch), emptying out the cigar ashes, tidying up the curtains, pretending to shake the rugs, and singing quietly to himself as he moved about, to some quaint old darky tune:

> "Oh, shall I be a dimmykrat,
> Or a Christian shall I be?
> Oh, shall I join de dimmykrats,
> And ne'er mah Lawd to see?"

when the door suddenly burst open, and in bounced Phil Gardiner, out of sorts from recitation after a dead flunk in mathematics (owing to political excitement), and slammed a lot of text-books on the table, saying:

"See here, John, I could n't find my razor this morning!"

"Your razzer, sah?"

"Yes, my new ivory-handled razor."

"Why, wy–wy–sah! I done fin' it fo' you, sah, right away, sah. Wha' ken it be, sah?"

"Honest John" looked dreamily out of the window.

"Well, get a move on you, then."

"Honest John, the thief," knew very well where it was. He had "borrowed" it for a man in the next entry. John never pinched anything for himself, but he never had the heart to deny his student employers anything. If one asked him for the moon, he'd have replied, "I'll try to git it fer you, sah," and go about snooping around in other men's rooms, trying to find a spare moon, if they happened to have one. Books, lamps, water pitchers, rugs, shirts, collars, razors, were always forthcoming if you demanded them of John, and the students got used to him and trusted him and his peculiar negro honesty, and called him "Honest John, the thief." One could be sure one's belongings never got away very far. "Honest John" never let them get away into another dormitory, for example; and ofttimes the scheme worked very well, *e.g.:* another man's razor is always sharper than one's own.

The razor, or *a* razor, came in with commendable promptness, and Phil began shaving contentedly before his glass, and "Honest John" finding that "Mr." Gardiner was unable to do much talking, did the talking himself, rather taking Phil at a disadvantage.

"You dimmykrats is a goin' fer to ruin dis country, sah, an' de fust ting I knows slavery 'll be 'stablished agin an' me an' my ole woman 'll hev to go down South an' work in de cottin feels; an' *I* don' mine ef de ole woman 's made fer ter go, but ef dey takes me away, dey takes an ole man what ain't good fer nothin' what wid rheumatiz, no sah! de old woman, she desarves fer to go back an' be a slave agin as she was bawn, down in So' Calina, yes, sah; fer she ain't fit fer to live, no s'haint."

"What 's the matter now, John?"

"What you tink of a woman put a chawm in her husban's tea fer to win back my love? Dat 's what she done! put yarbs in my tea, yes, sah. An' den when de chawm begun to wo'k, de fust pusson I sot eyes on was dat dere collud cook oveh to Professor Wistler's an' I done kiss dat cook soon 's I seen 'er, an' mah wife she seen me done it an' she pull mah wool, an' dere was a 'eep o' trouble fer me right den and dere; but dey 'll be more ef I jines de dimmykrats sah! an' I 'se in a 'eep of more trouble, wat wid Mistah Austin cain't find his new gold watch, sah, an' den Mistah Snow 'e says, ' John, ef you doan't brung back my smokin' jacket in one hour, I 'll thrash de skin off yo' old bones!' Dat wat 'e say, sah, an' Mistah Everson, sah, 'e's wearin' dat smokin' jacket, an' 'e says 'e likes it fuss rate, sah, fuss rate, an' do wat I ken, he won't take it off, sah; an' sometimes I *do* tink de good Lawd he done forgot po' John. Yes, I do, an' I tink dat ef de dimmykrats gits in pow' agin, de cullud folks might jess well turn up dere toes an' stop prayin',—an' den on top everythin' else I hearn tell dat Jefferson Davis, he want dead yit,—is dat so, Mistah Gardner?"

"Who told you that, John?" asked Phil, laughing.

"Dat 's wat several gentleums tole me. An' John Halter he said so too, dat he *reely* want dead, an' ef de dimmykrats git de pow' agin, a sekin time, dat dey 'll mak old Jeff Davis de reel president an' dat de cullud folks haid better look scace."

" Honest John " looked so seriously anxious

that Gardiner had not the heart to impose upon him.

"No, John," he said kindly. "Jeff Davis is really dead, and you darks are just as safe under a democratic *regime* as a republican. You can join the procession to-night and I'll get you a beautiful red cape and a lantern."

"Oh, no, sah. I ain't afraid, sah, but de cullud gentleums up mah way, sah, dey carry razzers, sah."

Gardiner laughed, but said nothing.

The old negro began laughing again in a moment. "Oh, ef de dimmykrats won't do nuffin' till me an' de ole woman is under groun,' why den, I don' keer what dey does."

"The democratic party will take better care of the negro than the republicans have ever thought of doing!" said Phil, with a grand flourish of his razor.

"Honest John" dodged to one side.

"T-t-take keer, Mistah Gard'ner, fo' de Lawd's sake, dat razzer's sharp! dat's Mistah Belcher's razzer, an' he tink a heap o' his razzer, sah, an' keeps hit mos' sharp as my ole woman's tongue, sah!"

"Well, John, you thief, return Tom Belcher

In the Political Cauldron. 47

his razor at once (Phil had finished shaving), and go find mine; if it is n't here in five minutes, I don't know but I'll force you to carry a lantern in our democratic procesh to-night."

But "Honest John, the thief," had quietly left the room.

Phil Gardiner inherited from his father the congressman, and his grandfather the governor, and his great-grandfather the high something or other, a rabid taste for politics. It was through Phil's ingenuity that, when class deacons were elected in Freshman year, and only seventy-nine were present, *his* favorite candidate received ninety-seven votes, and was duly elected! Phil had been on every conceivable kind of a committee, and had engineered every conceivable kind of a scheme through the class, from voting to wear silk hats the third term Freshman, and dropping a monster paper balloon with the class numeral on Prex's head from the top gallery at the Glee Club concert Prom. week, to electing the committee of the Senior Prom. He was very popular in his class, and very naturally was made chief marshal in the great monster procession in honor of Cleveland and Stevenson which was to come off that night, and which was calculated to throw utterly in the shade the republican procession a few nights before, and about which, owing to the most excellent and talented drum-major the democrats happened to possess in the person of one "Sodger" Flynn, a valiant Junior, there was already considerable talk on the Campus.

The republicans had a drum-major—Saxton, —but he was very rank in comparison with "Sodger" Flynn. He was n't in the same class with Flynn. He could twirl his baton after a fashion, but the hoodlums and street gamins followed the "Sodger" from York Square to the boat-house, fascinated by his wonderful manœuvres, and the independent voter of New Haven was naturally overawed and brought down and captured at once by the phenomenal twists and gyrations of Flynn's baton. He would throw it up in the air and catch it behind him, and twist it under his arms, his legs, and around his neck amid the shouts of the populace. Oh, it was a grand sight to see the "Sodger" lead the band around a corner, and file and counter-file past any obstruction, never out of step, and holding his head up proud and as if sure of victory! Ah, yes! Flynn was indeed the very heart and soul of the procession.

Imagine, therefore, Phil Gardiner's utter consternation when, just as he finished shaving, a little note was brought to him which he tore open and read, as follows:

"1282 FARNAM, October 28th.
"DEAR GARDINER—I am very sorry to say that I won't be able to march to-night. While I was fooling out in the gym. lot this morning, I sprained my ankle badly. The doctor says I won't walk for a week, perhaps two. I'm awful sorry.
"Yours truly,
"H. J. FLYNN.
"P. S.—You can have my baton if you wish it, but I'm sorry you can't have me.   F."

"Blankety blank blank!" said Phil, disgusted. "The 'Sodger' can't march!—sprained his ankle!"

A number of fellows had dropped in after morning recitation, and among them "Little Jack" Horner and "Boots" Paige, who were republicans by paternal choice.

"That's all right," said Horner; "you're dished—your procession won't amount to a hill of beans, without the 'Sodger'!"

"Blankety blankety—confound the little Irish fool! Could n't he wait and break his leg or even his neck *after* to-night, I should like to know? Now I 'm going over to his room and satisfy my mind it is n't a fake. Sprain his ankle! some republican has 'done' him on purpose! What the deuce are we to do for a drum-major?"

Phil rushed out of the room and over to Farnam, where the "Sodger" lived, and those in the room fell to discussing foot-ball, a favorite topic just then among some men for whom politics did not have an overpowering fascination.

Presently Phil came charging back again, very much harassed in mind.

"He can't move for a fact, poor devil!" he said. "Bad sprain,—but what am I to do? No one else can do the drum-major act, and the 'publicans 'll have the laugh on us!"

"Can't you get one in town,—hire one?"

"We have spent our last red in the band and the torches and the capes. We can't hire one,—it's a disgrace to us not to have our own drum-major! What luck!"

"Little Jack" Horner sat very quietly puffing away on a Nile cigarette. At last he said: "I guess I can fix it."

OSBORN HALL.

In the Political Cauldron.   51

"What do you mean, Jack?"

"Can you borrow the 'Sodger's' baton?"

"Yes, I think I can."

"Send for it, and I'll show you how to do the trick."

"Little Jack" Horner, as has been said, was a republican by parental influence, and the repubs. in the room all said: "You're not going to help the democrats out with their procesh, Jack?"

"You wait," said "Little Jack," and then he seemed to grin all over his round, Cupid-like little body, and they knew something was in the wind.

Phil Gardiner sent over and borrowed Flynn's baton, a very elegant affair with red tassels and brass head-piece. Gardiner and Flynn had "prepared" together at a military school on the Hudson, and the boys had presented the staff to the "Sodger" as a reward of distinguished merit on his leaving school for college. Flynn kept it carefully and sacredly in a long oaken box, one of the greatest treasures of his room.

He had great reluctance in lending the baton to Phil Gardiner, but his scruples were overcome by thoughts of doing some service to his party.

"Be careful of it, boys, I would n't lose it for a thousand dollars," he said from the couch where he lay with his sprained ankle in his Farnam room. "It 's my one trick I do which gives me hopes of immortality."

When "Little Jack" Horner got the baton in his hands, he called for some rubber bands, and knotted a half dozen of these together and fastened the end to the middle of the baton, and the other end to his wrist.

"Now watch me, and I 'll show you how the trick is done, Phil," he said, and he proceeded to astonish the roomful by his manipulations. He tossed the stick in the air and caught it; whirled it around twice (breaking a gas globe, but that did n't matter), and Phil Gardiner fairly danced with joy.

"You 're a little brick, Jack!" he cried. "Give it to me, and I 'll see what I can do with it."

Phil seized the baton, and did better than "Little Jack"—he broke a looking-glass!

Phil Gardiner practised all the morning and afternoon between recitations with the baton, and by evening felt that he would make an excellent substitute for the "Sodger." Whatever he did with the stick, and no matter how many times it came back and hit him on the head, he never lost it, and although he had terrific bumps on his forehead, which compelled him to wear his wide-a-wake cap on one side, and had received black and blue spots from "the d——d thing," as he called it, all over his arms and his body, he ate a hasty supper at his club and went over to High Street, where the student brigade—a force of some five hundred men—was to form, in capital spirits.

The procession was an imposing affair. Nearly two thousand good Democrats from New Haven and outlying towns were to march in it, and many houses and stores along Chapel Street and York, and through the city on the line of march, were brilliantly illuminated with red fire and Chinese lanterns. As the student force rested along High Street, waiting for the procession to come down Chapel from York Street, it was seen that each class carried a large banner and illumination: "Cleveland and Reform," "Free Trade and Cheap Commodities," "Yale and Reform," "'Umpty-Six and

Cleveland," "Grandpa's Hat is in the Soup," and a lot more mottoes hurling contumely upon the enemy, printed in staring black letters.

Phil Gardiner combined marshal duties with that of drum-major, and he hurried down the line giving commands, and the student ranks were arranged six abreast. The Seniors came first, then the Juniors, Sophs., and Freshmen. Then followed the Sheffs. with a separate band, with a modest drum-major of their own.

Phil had borrowed a shako of a New Haven friend—a member of the "Grays,"—and as he heard the head band of the procession, with trumpets and drums, marching into Chapel at York Street corner, he suddenly conceived a brilliant plan—he determined to execute a grand *coup* of strategy and place his own command at the right of the entire procession!

So, ordering his band to strike up, he at once gave the command to march, and wheeled his columns to the left, past the Art building down Chapel, the line of march at the head of the procession.

Of course, this tickled the students immensely and they gave the college cheer, while Major O'Dowd, who was in command, leading the procession of townies down Chapel from York, on horseback, was naturally furious.

"Begorra! ut's a student thrick!" he cried to his aids, and dashed down toward the student brigade to head them off. But Phil Gardiner was proudly leading off the band and twirling and tossing his baton in the air, to the delight of the crowds on the sidewalks, and the Major had to turn back discomfited.

"I'll be even wid the likes of you yet, Misther Gardner!" bawled the Major, shaking his sword in the air, but he had to halt his command to allow the students first place.

Down Chapel they marched, the band playing Sousa's "High-School Cadet Two-Step," and Phil Gardiner leading on, tossing his baton, whirling it about his shako, catching it again with the greatest ease and agility,— it was the proudest moment of his life.

"Little Jack" Horner and a lot of Junior and Senior republicans had gathered on the Osborne Hall steps to guy the procession as they went by.

"Get on to the fake drum-major!" shouted the republicans, but it did n't go with the crowd for a cent.

"Gad!" said Paige, "Jack, your improvised drum-major is a howling success!" as Gardiner, feeling on his mettle between the mass of republican students on one side, and the New Haven House, whose windows and balconies were crowded with girls, on the other, gave his baton an extra toss and won the applause and hand-clapping as he came along, the very model of a modern drum-major.

"Watch him, watch him!" cried "Little Jack," excitedly. "If that rubber elastic breaks he's dished!"

Then, as luck would have it, as he said the words, the baton in Phil's hands gave a tremendous leap and landed far on the turf of the common, behind the crowd, amid the laughter of all.

"He's done! He's done, boys! Run get that baton!" shouted "Little Jack," to his alert republican friends. Barrington dashed swiftly through the crowd, grabbed the baton out of the hands of a gamin who had picked it up, and ran madly across the common, until he was out of sight; then he carried it up to "Sodger" Flynn's room and stood it up against his door and sneaked back through the Campus to Osborn Hall.

In the Political Cauldron. 57

Phil Gardiner gave a cry of despair, seized his shako off his head, tucked it under his arm, and, forgetting his duties as drum-major, started madly after his lost baton. They were then just at the corner of Chapel and College Streets, —the famous "fence corner" so admirably depicted in Howland's painting, now in the gymnasium. The band, seeing Drum-Major Gardiner turn to the left, in the blind, fatuous way bands have (they follow their drum-major like sheep), wheeled to the left also, and led the procession of student torches idiotically off past the colleges down College toward Elm.

Phil Gardiner, seeing this mistake, halted his column a moment, then, seeing that the jig was up, and that the baton was gone and "forever lost," seized a torch and marched his men on down College Street, swearing that he'd have revenge on somebody, he hardly knew whom.

Major O'Dowd, greatly pleased to get even, resumed the leadership, and marched *his* column down Chapel, the prescribed line of march, thus making two fine democratic displays on either side of the green, and giving an impression to the casual looker-on as if the whole thing had been so planned from the beginning.

Well, those two democratic processions kept it up all night pretty much, wandering over the lower part of New Haven, a "fairly perfect example of the usual dissensions in the democratic party," as the republican newspapers hinted next day. But one thing was to their credit,—they never came to blows, and the display was really magnificent.

"All's well that ends well." President Cleveland, I believe, is at present occupying the White House at Washington, and Phil Gardiner has hanging in his boarding-house room in New York, where he is at present studying law, as a preliminary to entering politics in his native State, a handsome baton with a silver head, presented to him by his democratic classmates and friends, as a testimonial of their regard for his efforts in the great political campaign generally, that year, and particularly for his brave effort to do drum-major's duty with an elastic string.

"LITTLE JACK" HORNER'S PIE.

"How did you get jugged, 'Little Jack'?"

"I did n't," he answered indignantly, "besides, that 's a very impertinent question to ask of any gent as considers hisself a gent. It is begging the question; it 's as bad as that funny one—oh! so funny—in Jevons's *Logic*, 'Why did you kill your grandmother?'—the joke we all laughed so hard over, by preconcerted signal, don't you remember in recitation last term?"

"Tell us the whole story; we were in at the end of it; we each had a piece of pie."

They were sitting and smoking on the fence in front of Durfee. It was a mild June evening. They were in the midst of the usual discussion about the crew or the nine. Wherever a knot of students gathered at this season, on the Campus, the subject of excited conversation was the nine; if it was n't, it was the crew. If it was neither the nine nor the crew, it was the class nine or crew. If it was neither class nine nor crew, it was, probably, Harvard's nine or crew. You see, the student topics of conversation at this season, after the secret-society elections had been given out, and there was little to look forward to, on the whole, were rather limited.

"Little Jack" Horner puffed away on his cigarette, smiled, looked knowing, said nothing. Then he climbed up laboriously—he was too short to do it comfortably—and perched on the fence.

Austin, "Laze" Aldrich, Barrington, Tad Nelson, and "Boots" Paige were in the group.

"Haley can't pitch for a tinker's——," said Austin.

"Shut up! Let's hear 'Little Jack's' account of himself."

They enjoyed "Little Jack" Horner's tales, even if, dear reader, they may not always be agreeable to you, an outsider. His manner was everything. He'd wink his eye, roll his tongue, drawl, imitate the speakers, and keep every one laughing, although they might have heard the tale a dozen times.

"This happened last Friday night," said

"Little Jack" Horner, "and it's too fresh to be given away yet. It must be kept on the dead quiet, for if the Faculty knew it,—my marks are now about the limit. Barrington, when dining with Prexy next Sunday, don't tell it as an after-dinner yarn, for I want very much, if I can, to lap over into Junior year with 'youse fellers.'"

"Go ahead, 'Jack' Horner!"

After lighting a fresh cigarette, and tipping his hat on the back of his head, "Little Jack" went ahead as follows:

"Hurlburt, 'Handsome Dan,' Billy Scot, and I were over at the club, and, like a pack of fools having nothing else to do, got to drinking cow punches.

"Now, we didn't know anything about milk punches, as you will find out if you listen. But they are awfully dangerous food. We drank a round, then another round. Then we couldn't think of the name of any other kind of drink, and had 'just one more,' and,—I don't know; we all went up to my room. Then we went back to the club, like a pack of fools, and bet each other we couldn't go one more; then we had two more each, and then we went back to my room in Lawrance, and all went to sleep. Yes, sir, it was about seven then,—without thinking about supper at all. We lay down in our tracks just as we were, and when my chum Keith came in after supper, he just said 'Gee!' and walked out again and let us sleep, and we slept; and Keith he spent the night over with 'Dwarf' Sprague in Durfee.

"Well, we slept an' slept, and along about five o'clock in the morning we began to wake up, and I felt deuced hungry.

"Then, by Jerusalem, a funny thing happened. You see, the milk had all digested by this time and left the rum and brandy room to get in its fine work in their heads; and Hurlburt was under a frightful jag, and 'Handsome Dan' Hastings was going about on his hands and knees looking, he said, for his lost virtue. Billy Scot tipped over all the chairs and threw my Greek lexicon out of the window. I was the only sober man in the crowd."

"Oh, oh, how about bawling for your mammy —calling to the night-watchman, out of the window, 'Go up, thou baldhead!'" cried Trowbridge; "and 'Watchman, tell us of the night?'"

"Shut up. Who's telling this yarn? I saw it wouldn't do to let 'em fool around and make any more noise in college, so I got 'em all out on a foot race, for a purse. I started 'em all up towards Sheff. and Hillhouse Avenue, on a dead run. The usually fastidious Hurlburt took the gutter and fell down three times on the way to Sheff.! Then I think we serenaded a fem. sem. and the next thing—queer, wasn't it?—we found ourselves solemnly sitting in a row, on the steps of Osborne Hall, and hardly a sign of a jag between us!

"By that time, say six o'clock in the morning, we were mortal hungry, and nothing was open, for we'd tried several joints on the way up and they were closed tight as drums.

"We were wondering what we'd do or wait for breakfast, when, to our immense relief, up drove the great covered wagon of the 'Great Consolidated American Pie Company,' whatever that was, and delivered a dozen pies at the restaurant.

"We felt in our pockets but had n't a cent between us, and Billy Scot, when the pie-man got off his perch and went in to deliver his 'goods,' slipped into the covered wagon, and crooked four pies, and got back without the driver's seeing him. Gee! they were daisies too! 'Easy fruit!' we all said, and the driver in the Company's uniform, seeing us eating his pies, looked mad, and shook his fist at us. We gave him a little chin—I remember Hurlburt's asking him if he was anything like the Pied Piper of Hamelin? and the fellow swore a round of first-rate oaths—'Blankety blankety blank you blankety students, I'll get even with you yet!'

"'Go there yourself!' We laughed and munched and he drove off furiously, down Chapel Street. We thought that was the last we should see of him.

"But no sooner had we finished our pies in good shape, and were just about ready for another fresh one, when back came the 'Great Consolidated' again, and the driver got out and went into the restaurant just as before.

"Gee! I could n't stand that, you know; so, being frightfully hungry by this time, I sneaked up to the wagon, and climbed in to pinch some more pies. I got up on the forward wheels and was just climbing over the seat into the interior of the 'cavern' as our friend Virgil observes of the interior of the Wooden Horse at Troy, when—Christopher Hemlock! Two coppers grinning like a pair of bloomin' hyenas jumped forward, grabbed me by the arm and pulled me over the wheels and into the inside of that awful pie-wagon, where it was dark as pitch. It had a door which shut tight, and you can imagine my feelings to be shut up in that horrible Black Maria, with two policemen and forty thousand pies! There were apple-pies and cranberry-pies, and meat-pies and custard-pies, and, although I was still hungry, I had enough pie—and it was awful! and what's more, I trembled, for I knew if the Faculty got wind of it I'd be sent down sure—yes, it would have been three months *in rure*.

"Well, I cussed and blanked 'em, but the coppers held on to me all the harder and tighter, and we bounced and bounded from one side of the street to the other inside the 'Consolidated,' in our mad haste to get to the jug.

"Of course, I could n't see what went on outside the blamed pie-wagon, but I knew that Hurlburt and Dan and Billy Scot were n't the chappies to let me be whirled off to the jug without some sort of a feeble protest. So I just kept the coppers interested; although I heard some sort of scuffling going on with the driver, I did n't know what it was,—I kept the bobbies busy with me, and drew their attention away.

"Presently the bloomin' pie-wagon stopped, then there seemed to be more scuffling outside and I fought and tore trying to get out, and then the wagon went on again.

"Then it came to a full stop, and they opened the door of the cussed thing and out we got in front of the jug. How he did it I don't know, but there, sitting on the driver's box as cool as Moses, and in the driver's uniform and cap, sat Billy Scot, as big as life. What they'd done with the real driver, I did not know till later.

"'Keep 'em busy and they won't notice me,' he whispered, and I began to pull and haul and pretend I was going to break away and skip across the green up to the Campus.

"'For a leetel divvil,—yer a corker!' said one of the cops. 'Kape still, or I'll use me club as a persuader! Yiz stoodents 'ill find out soon yiz doant own de eart!'

"'I would n't want to own "de eart" on you!' I retorted.

"In we all went before the police captain,

and as it was then only about half-past six o'clock, the captain was just out of bed and hardly awake, and in a state of rage at having so early an arrest to attend to.

"'Wha' 's the charge?' he growled, as we all lined up before the bar, I with a cop on either side holding on to my arm for dear life (I think I came up to their elbows), and Billy Scot in the Great Consolidated Pie Company's uniform, cap and coat, and looking as innocent as a sheep.

"'Wha' 's the charge, officer?' growled the captain, a huge Irishman, with a red face and bleary eye.

"'Stealin' pies,—he's the driver [indicating Scot with a jerk of his thumb],—he makes the charge, captain.'

"'Do you make the charge?' said the captain, looking at Scot fixedly, as if to bore a hole through him."

"'Agin' who?' said Billy, in a surly tone,— Billy was adapting himself to look at things from the driver's standpoint.

"'Agin' this young man they have here.'

"'*He* wa' n't stealin' no pies,' said Billy, lurching forward.

"'Well,—who was then?' bellowed the captain.

"'Them two officers, captain. An' it ain't the fust time nayther.'

"The two officers at this became absolutely dumb and speechless with astonishment. I never saw any one so nonplussed in all my life! But I held myself in and kept myself down and said: 'That's so, Captain Cockran—[I knew his name]. They got caught and tried to lay the blame on an innocent man.'

"One of the coppers, in a sort of apoplectic coma, stammered something, and the captain bawled out, in a voice of fury: 'Howld yer tongue! will yez! Wait till I ask yez to spake! It's time this petty thavin' by officers should be stopped, an' I mane to stop ut ef it takes all the min off the force!'

"'They was inside my pie-wagon,' said Scot.

"'They was? Was you inside the pie-wagin?' demanded the captain, in a voice of thunder. 'Spake!'

"'Yis,' answered one of the coppers, meekly terrified at his captain's sternness.

"'Thin,——I'll hear no more o' this. Distcharge that little bye there as looks as inner-cent as a new-born babe!'

"I took a step backward.

"'Officer, arrist these two roundsmen, an' lock them up until a complaint ken be made out agin' them before the justice.'

"'Yer Honor,' said Billy Scot, 'I don't wish to press no charge,—I jest want the officers reprimanded,—that's all.'

"I thought myself it was all he could or ought to expect at the time!

"The captain, in his outraged sense of justice, would n't let either of the men speak and clear himself, and proceeded to give them a fearful raking down, and at the close of his tongue lashing remanded them over to be further lectured by the Justice, who usually opened court at ten A.M.

"So Billy and I thanked the captain, and went out grinning all over, and got on the seat of the pie wagon and drove off up towards the colleges, laughing until the tears ran down our cheeks.

"'Where have you hid the driver?' I asked Billy.

"'They said they'd take him up to the

room, but I advised them to keep him down in the basement, and be careful about names too. You see we had to drag him off the seat, and we mauled him pretty well in doing it. Then we made him take off his coat, and I put it on,—and you know the rest. The last *I* saw of the driver, he was being led, against his better judgment, at a fast pace toward Lawrance Hall!'

"So we drove the pie-wagon up Elm to the corner of College Street, and Scot held the reins while I went in to investigate.

"Hurlburt whistled to me out of his Lawrance window, and told me they had the driver up in the room, so I ran up, and found they had the driver tied to the steam radiator!

"'He threatens to peach on us,' said Dan.

"'Does he?' said I. 'Well, then, we'll have all the fun we can now, boys!' And I got out a large sheet of paper and marked on it, in big letters:

> FRESH PIES FREE TO-DAY ONLY!!

And the driver saw the sign and weakened a little, I thought. So I said: 'We'll put this sign on the wagon and drive in on the Campus. In three minutes every fellow in college will have a piece of pie!'

"'What's more,' said Scot, 'we'll dispose of you—O pie driver—in a dungeon cell underground where no pies will ever cheer your chary soul again!'

"The driver turned very pale, and trembled.

"'Say,' he pleaded, 'don't put me into one o' them jugs without no windys to 'em, will ye?—they calls 'em Bones 'n Keys.'

"'No,' laughed Scot, 'we won't do that!'

"But the driver gave no further sign of weakening and said nothing, and so I ran down, and Scotty and I determined to have a little fun. It was near chapel time now, and every one was up, and going or coming from breakfast. We drove the great van up between Durfee and Alumni Hall, and enjoyed ourselves immensely perambulating up and down in front of Farnam and Lawrance, with our sign out in full force. I don't think I ever had so much fun in all my life. Scotty got a fishhorn from somewhere, and the procession fell in behind the wagon, and we marched over almost as far as the Art building, when Professor Dribble came up to us and ordered us off the Campus.

"'Who owns that vehicle?' he asked.

"'The Great Consolidated American Pie Company,' I answered.

"'What are you doing with that vehicle on the Campus, Mr. Horner?'

"'Only going to prayers, sir,' said Scotty, and I spoke up quickly:

"'I'm trying to turn it around and get out, sir.'

"'See that you do so without further delay!'

"Then he turned and walked away, looking very angry.

"Then I described a conic section, and drove around past the library and so got back to Durfee. There the 'Dwarf' and his gang of Durfee turks set upon us, and then the whole college had pie! Scotty and I could n't stop them,—it was no use. Every pie in the wagon was captured! One hundred and fifty pies stolen! Oh, the slaughter was awful! Even Seniors went crazy with the rest and daubed themselves over with pie. The chapel bell began tolling—and pie invaded the sanctuary. We called a sweep and told him to hold the horses, and hurried into prayers, and when we came out every dark on the Campus was around that pie-wagon like flies around molasses. I ran up to Hurlburt's room and tried to get in, but the door was locked, and I heard the driver inside begging to be let out, and swearing he'd never tell a soul about the affair.

"'But I'm a worryin' myself fer fear them nigs 'll eat all the paint off my new waggin,' he said, gazing out the window 'an' them 'osses may be et too—oh, this is too much! Please, kind gents, let me go! let me go home to mother!'

"Well, the upshot of it was that Hurlburt, Dan, and Scotty came up at that moment, and we went out and borrowed some money, made up a purse of twenty dollars on the spot, and the driver at last was more than satisfied. He'd sold his pies at a big profit, and he went and got his team and meekly drove off.

"I forgot to say that we warned the driver if he ever did anything about it we'd have his life!"

"Well, I hope nothing will ever come of it!" said the listeners, laughing.

And nothing ever did, for the "Great Consolidated American Pie Company," which probably consisted of the driver, his wife, mother, and all the driver's family, wrote "Little Jack" a pleasant letter a few days later, and sent him a huge apple-pie, two and a half feet in diameter, by actual measurement. They could hardly get it in his room door! It is needless to say that Hurlburt, "Handsome Dan," Billy Scot, Keith, and "Boots" Paige, and several more, had a royal feast out of it, and later on they mixed a punch, and all sang in maudlin chorus, at about two o'clock in the morning, to the horror of the tutor beneath them:

> " Little Jack Horner,
> Sat in a corner,
> Eating his Great American Pie;
> He put in his thumb,
> And pulled out a plum,
> And said: 'Oh, what a great boy am I!'"
>
> *(Repetitio ad infin.)*

WITH THE DWIGHT HALL HEELERS.

AVERILL came up to his room in South Middle with somewhat more than his usual appearance of quietude and dejection. He was tall, thin, and stooped a little, with that melancholy droop to his shoulders which proclaims a man recklessly given over to the making the very most of his college course, and possessing a devotion to midnight oil and dull grinding which must inevitably lead to a philosophical and incapacitate him for the boat or the foot-ball field,—as Barrington said of his kind. His face was drawn and pale and as he entered the door his lustrous dark eyes, in which the beautiful soul of the man shone out with the fine enthusiasm of a true Grecian, looked anywhere but into the eyes of his chum.

Averill sank down in a corner of his lounge, and looked blankly into the embers of the wood fire for a moment, then rose with a curious restlessness, and stood with his hands in his pockets before the window, looking down at a number of his classmates who were standing on the sidewalk laughing and joking about something that apparently had recently amused them.

His chum, known to a majority of the class as a "greasy grind,"—"Deacon" Demarest,—had raised his eyes and glanced at Averill through a pair of near-sighted spectacles, and let them drop again on the *Agricola*, of one Caius Cornelius Tacitus, a work he was studiously perusing by way of doing a little extra reading for a classical scholarship prize. The examination was to take place two weeks later, and the good Deacon for a month had assumed the usual "grouch" of a hard-working "dig." He was nervous, peevish, irritable, and unhappy. If he should be fortunate enough to be successful he would be able to finish his course without further drawing upon the narrow store of funds possessed by his widowed mother. Ah, how the good fellow longed, toiled, and *prayed* to be successful! Aye—he even went so far that he thought it no sin to read Epictetus Sunday afternoons instead of going down to the usual mission!

The Deacon was already working extra hours for his prize scholarship exams., and Averill had been for a week particularly careful not to disturb him, and particularly anxious to give to his chum the aid and assistance of his own more brilliant scholarship. The "digs." to a man had been confident that Averill could have the scholarship almost for the asking, but Averill, when the time came, seemed too listless to enter the competition, and evidently preferred his chum's ambitions to his own. For a week he had done no reading for it,— indeed he had done little or no work of any kind. He had gone into recitation after recitation entirely unprepared, and once or twice narrowly escaped making a disgraceful fizzle.

The Deacon had warned his chum and had taken him seriously to task for his singular lapse from his usual studious habits. But his short, sharp admonitions to return to the path of rectitude had been lost on Averill, who seemed at times so ill, so enervated, and so depressed that the good Deacon almost feared he was about to come down with a fever.

But a man cramming heart and soul for a severe examination, working steadily eighteen hours out of the twenty-four, is the most utterly selfish being in the world. His strain and stress of mind bent on the accumulation of details, and the filling the storehouse of his memory with an enormous variety of unnecessary facts, which he is to use once and forget ever afterward, compel him to concentrate all his forces upon himself, and to forget his friends and his surroundings.

Deacon Demarest had a nervous irritated sense that all was not well with Averill, but the overpowering feeling was of high indignation that at a time so trying to him, his chum should seize the opportunity to have such distress. Averill's very self-repression, his silence, his occasional sighs, made the Deacon break out once or twice raging,—as men will savagely growl who have had too little sleep and too much nervous strain for a fortnight. How could he gather in the fine points of the *Cyropædia*, or master the profound meaning of the *Œdipus Tyrannus*, or pursue his Quintus Curtius, knowing and feeling the burden of his chum's unuttered, and apparently unutterable, sorrow?

Two men living so closely together as chums in college act and react on each other, profoundly, like man and wife. Averill endured these outbreaks without a murmur. Sometimes he absented himself for long periods; sometimes he expressed himself sententiously in his brief phrase, τό ἐπιτιμᾶν ῥᾴδιον ἐστιν —to find fault is easy,—but never resented Demarest's nervous bitterness; once he put his hand quietly on Demarest's shoulder and gently patted it. It brought the moisture to the "Deacon's" near-sighted old eyes, and brought him abruptly to his feet, with a sigh and a "God forgive my outrageous temper!" Then he 'd shake Averill's hand heartily, and Averil would sit staring at him with his dark speaking eyes, full of affection and full of strange dread, listless and inert.

Demarest looked up and said suddenly, one day: "There 's a secret, Bob, which lies heavy on your heart; I have felt the burden of it for days; but the exam., Bob—"

"I know; and it will keep!"

"You will tell me?"

"Yes, after your trouble is over, old boy."

"If you cared to tell me *now*, perhaps it would be better, I should n't be worried."

"No, there is time enough."

The Deacon looked at his chum for a moment, then plunged into his Plato, with a sigh, and a grit of his teeth. If there was any one in the world, he wondered, so unselfish, so considerate as his chum? But *his* business *now* was with the profane old pagans, and, well, he remembered that Bob's secret would keep.

And the secret?

Averill with a half dozen "Dwight Hall heelers," as they were called by the Paige-Horner-Barrington crowd—the swell crowd,— ran a little mission in the lower part of the city, a mission which, as some of these devoted Christians began to feel, seemed to be hardly more than a resting-place each Sunday for the lowest order of the species tramp. The good they did, the words they spoke, of how little effect! It was almost heart-breaking sometimes, to see the same old "bums," after trying more or less, to lead a better life, come tumbling down again into the gutter, and be forced to be lifted up once more by main strength and hard praying! Averill seemed to understand the poor lost creatures better than any one else. It was never his habit to rebuke or admonish or talk down to them. He'd simply speak to them as if he were down there in the mire with them, struggling upwards with them, he and they together; he'd say it was hard to give up the drink, and sigh, just as if he himself felt it as keenly true as they, poor wretches.

"Ah, my lads," said "Little Jack" Horner, who, one day, with "Boots" Paige strolled into the mission to be amused and came away very silent and much impressed, and related what they had seen, in "Laze" Aldrich's room. "Ah, my lads, if you could have heard that fine Grecian, the best Greek scholar by a thousand yards in the class, far away and beyond anything *I* ever supposed possible; have you heard Averill in the *Antigone?* Well, I've heard him in the *Antigone* and I've heard him speaking to half a dozen old 'bums.' It was n't eloquence, it was something higher. They'd been drunk for a week, and turned up at the mission because it was warm, and they got a cup of hot coffee and a biscuit, and Bob Averill spoke to them. 'Boots' and I sat riveted in our seats."

There was a short pause.

"Little Jack" seemed strangely agitated, and they told him to go right on and not get into a funk.

"If he had been inspired, he would have spoken just so. Temperance?"—"Little Jack" made a contemptuous face. "No, no; it was something like this, but I can't give you the tenderness, the gentleness, the real goodness of it. 'We have a hard life, have n't we, friends?—and we drink to get out of it; life is what we are trying to get away from, and life is bitter, cruel, and hard to most of us; we've had our troubles, God knows; no shelter over our heads some of these cold nights, and the drink is shelter; no coats to keep the cold out, drink is a sort of overcoat for a time; we remember some happy days in the past: we had a home once,—the drink makes us not care for them now; we remember a woman's pleading face, mother or wife; oh, the drink drowns out that sweet face too! We forget, we don't care; then comes the memory of a little child we once held in our arms,—*our* little child, and it laughed as we held it. Oh! the drink drowns out all recollection of the day we held it and it died in our arms; and the drink is a good thing, it makes us forget, and it takes us out of life; and if we were good workmen once, the drink makes us glad we're out of it, out of work, out of everything, out of life. And so may we not just as well die? Let us not care for those who are near to us,—let us drink,—get more drink,—more drink,—and so out of life and into the night of nights. . . .' The hobos hung on his words as if they were golden ducats; I never saw anything like it,—so inexpressibly mournful,—so hopeless,—so tearless; then an expression of joy and peace leapt into his fine intellectual face. 'But no! I say,— I can't die yet! I don't want to die! I want life,—but the right kind. I want happiness—a home. All I had once, everything.—as it was; I want life,—as it was, as it was!'

"'How can this be done?' Then of course, he gave 'em religion, hot and strong, and the pledge on top of it."

"Little Jack" persuaded a number of fellows to go down to the mission the Sunday following, and hear Averill.

"Now, if he doesn't persuade you chaps to sign the pledge in fifteen minutes, I'm a liar." said "Little Jack."

Aldrich said: "Well, I hope we may get our money's worth. I'm giving up a half-promised call on some easy people, who are always at home Sunday afternoon."

"Yes, I hope it's all you and 'Boots' say it is," yawned Keith, as he rose to put on his overcoat. "But I've never been in a regular 'bum' mission,—it must be rather amusing to see some of the old tramps on the anxious seat!"

"Any pretty girls go down there?" asked Aldrich, as they sauntered across the Campus toward Chapel Street.

"No," said Paige "It isn't a suitable place for the queens; it's run entirely by Dwight Hall heelers."

"I don't see what we are going down there for," laughed Keith.

"I assure you, Averill's talk to those fellows is wonderful!" said "Little Jack" earnestly. "You wait, and decide for yourselves."

"I'm afraid it's one of your jokes, 'Jack.'"

And they went on down the street.

The mission was pretty well crowded by the time the party got there. The day was damp and chilly, and an unpleasantly odorous steam arose from several old "bums" who had seated themselves close to the hot stove. A number of students were engaged in teaching some of the younger hoodlums, and Averill himself was seated in the centre of a class of tough-looking, ill-kempt women. The party entered and took seats at the rear of the hall, and presently Averill stepped up on the platform and gave out a hymn, reading a verse:

> "If through oft troubled seas
> Toward Heaven we calmly sail,
> Blest be the tempest, kind the storm,
> That drives us nearer home."

He seemed paler and more wretched than usual that day, as if some unusual tale of woe and sorrow had been confided to him,—more than he could bear. It was evident that the poor deluded tramps and worthies who tried, with quavering voices, to sing the hymn, looked up to Averill as they did to no other teacher in the mission. They pressed about him for his sympathy,—and his simple words which came so direct from his heart.

As the hymn closed, and the music of the melodeon died away, a scuffling noise was heard at the door, and loud shouts, as of boys in the street, accompanied by oaths and execrations, preceded the inrush of a collarless and hatless old tramp, evidently far gone with liquor. He wore an overcoat, dirty and covered with mud, as if he had been rolled over and over in the street, and had a cut over one eye which bled, and disfigured what might have been, under other circumstances, a fine, intellectual face. He burst into the hall and advanced, like some ugly wild animal, half way down the aisle toward the platform, where he paused and looked crazily around, and steadied himself against the back of a seat.

"Where's my son?—my son, they told me he was here?"

He rolled his bleary eyes around the room, and his unshaven, grizzly, bloody face took on an expression of almost diabolical hate.

"Where's my good son?—(hic)—my pet boy—my dawlin' s-son, who they say is such a wond'ful scholar? . . . I want him to c-come with me."

The stillness in the little hall was the stillness of death. Would any one respond to such a call? "Put him out!" cried a number of toughs near him, and rising ready to do so, if Mr. Averill should give the command.

THE ART BUILDING.

"Shell we bounce him, sir?" called out a seedy old bum, with a bob and curtsey toward Averill, who stood mutely staring at the intruder, as if in a trance. "Shell we do 'im up, as he 'd oughter be did up fer a tryin' fer ter bust de meetin'?"

"Say," said another bloated old derelict, who had floated without sail or rudder on life's tempestuous sea for many a long year. "Say, boss, le' me trow 'im out de winder, an' chuck 'im inter de nex' street. . . . 'E ain't no Christian,—no 'e ain't. 'E ain't no Christian, such as us!"

"Bounce de kite!" screamed a sodden-looking woman, with long, bedraggled hair. "'E 's ready fer a scrap, 'e is. . . . 'E ain't no Christian! 'E orter be fired, so 'e ort!"

"Jump on de bloke wid yer two feet," bawled another tramp. "An' trod 'im down! 'E ain't no Christian, like as us! 'E don't git no carfy 'ere!"

Suddenly, Averill straightened himself up, then to the astonishment and consternation of all in the room, stretched out his hands.

"*Father! Oh, my poor father!*" he cried, in agony, and his head sunk in his hands.

Aldrich, Paige, and "Little Jack" were on their feet with excitement. They saw Averill go to meet the intruder; they saw the latter draw back as if to strike him; then they saw the drunken man reel and fall in a fit on the floor, his son bending over him.

Averill looked up with an expression of extreme humility.

"Friends," he said, with an unsteady voice, "this poor man is my own father,—once a kind heart, a good man,—once a student where I am now a student. . . . See what drink has brought to him—and to me! It has caused the death of my mother through sorrow; it has driven his friends from him—he has sunk down, down to utter ruin. My poor father! My own father—who used to carry me in his arms!"

The words were simple, spoken from the heart. To those who knew Averill they were profoundly touching. The cynical Aldrich was the first to go forward and help carry the lifeless body into an adjoining room, and "Little Jack" hurried out after a doctor. Other students kept the meeting in order and endeavored to utilize the episode for the benefit of the other poor victims of rum in the room.

Averill knelt over his father's body, chafing his hands and loosening his overcoat. It was seen that beneath it he wore only a begrimed red flannel shirt. They asked the son no questions after his father, they only pressed his hand in sympathy.

"Little Jack" soon returned with a doctor, who, as soon as he had restored the drunkard to consciousness, rang for an ambulance and had him taken to the hospital.

"It's a bad case of alcoholism," said the doctor, as the ambulance drove rapidly away. But with rest and quiet he may recover. You seem to take a special interest in this case, Mr. Averill?"

"Oh, we all do," put in "Little Jack," quickly. "I will gladly do all I can to get the poor man on his feet again."

"These fellows are hard to cure," said the doctor. "Temptation stands beckoning to them at every street corner."

Poor Averill sighed and looked down. "I think I will walk over to the hospital, fellows," he said, quietly. "He will be glad to have me near him, perhaps——"

"If such a man could be kept in an asylum

for a few years or, better, sent on a long sea voyage——"

"A sea voyage! Why, that's dead easy fruit; I'll write to *my* father," huskily said "Boots" Paige, who had been very silent.

Averill looked up quickly at the emphasis he put on the "my." He caught the friendliness of it and the tears sprang into his eyes.

"God knows how kind——" Then he turned away, quickly, and in a moment Averill had gone up the street with "Little Jack."

"Now, then," said Aldrich, *cum anctoritate*. "Not a word about all this in college." The other students, four Dwight Hall heelers, had come out, after locking the door of the meeting-house. "Paige and I will manage to get Averill's father out of town when he gets out of the hospital, and we'll make it a point to get him on a vessel. I knew a drunkard once who was cured by a sea voyage. Poor old Bob Averill —he's a trump,—I—I think I would have been coward enough to disown the old man——"

"So would I!" said Paige. "Think how Averill must have suffered!"

"For two weeks," spoke up one of the mission teachers, not a student, "the old drunkard has been here in town, begging and threatening his son. He has given his father, from time to time, money which was spent in rum. Poor Averill! His father threatened to make a scene on the Campus,—he was up there drunk one day, but Robert did not know of it,—he did not then proclaim his relationship,—for Averill's sake this had better be kept a secret."

The mission work of the "crowd" was so unaffectedly and tactfully done that Averill could not refuse it. Not a word was known of the old reprobate in College, and when Averill, "Boots" Paige, and "Little Jack," accompanied by a neatly-dressed, middle-aged invalid, went to New York two weeks later, not a soul was aware of their visit. They got old Averill on a sailing vessel bound for Japan, the captain of which was a sturdy teetotaler.

"Why, let him stay by the ship fer two years an' not taste it, an' he's sure to come out a free man!" he said heartily. "An' I mean to keep him at work too. No loafin' on *my* ship, not for no man! He shall do a lot of figgerin'—an' a leetel haulin', too,—yes, sir!"

Bob Averill's father was willing to go, and make a last effort to reform. They parted with affection, and young Averill went back to College much cheered in mind.

His chum, good Deacon Demarest, received him with a smile and a hearty slap on the back.

"I 've got the scholarship, Bob!—an' my mind 's at rest. I was a brute to you, old boy, all those weeks of cramming, forgive me, will you?"

Averill shook his hand heartily, his pure, sensitive face illumined with intense happiness. If any man's soul shone through his eyes, Averill's did. He had passed through the valley of the shadow, and come out safely on the other side.

"And now,—I 'm all through with worry and trouble—tell me yours." The Deacon's earnest face grew serious, and his voice dropped. "I am the closest friend you have, Bob. Tell me your secret?"

Averill thought a moment, then hesitated. Then his face broke into a radiant smile. "I have n't any secret now to tell, Deacon!"

Then they both stood a moment looking out of that old South Middle window, on the Campus, and down upon the throngs of students passing to and fro, upon one of the queer old sweeps laden with broom and dust-pan, upon the picture of noisy, busy, student life, and the Deacon, catching sight of Paige, "Little Jack" Horner, Aldrich, and a few of the "crowd," who were amusing themselves with snowballing each other, laughing and shouting, said sadly:

"I pity those easy-going fellows who are always in such high spirits, and who never think of the suffering which goes on about them; who never, even by accident, do any good to any one."

Averill interrupted quickly. "I don't think we do those fellows justice," he said. "Please don't say anything against them. I think I know them better than you."

THE "DWARF'S" PROM.

"Boots" Paige, "Tad" Nelson, "Great" Barrington, and "Laze" Aldrich were feeling fine as fiddles one Sunday afternoon in January. They had just finished lunch at the Club, which consisted largely of a "cold bot and hot lob," and Boots had drawn out of his case four large, long, and strong Invincibles and presented them, and they were enjoying their coffee and smoke, *cum dignitate*, and talking about the Prom. which was to come off the week following.

The general idea was, if possible, to get "Dwarf" Sprague into his evening suit, and to attend the Prom., and furthermore, if possible, get him spooney on some "queen," and have some fun out of him at the ball. There was a bottle for the successful persuader of Sprague.

While they were talking about him, as was the case with the devil, he entered the room, and sat down near them.

Dwarf Sprague, sometimes called "The Honest," confessed that he had once been partially taught to dance by a certain cousin, and that after an exhaustive effort one evening, she had asked him if he imagined he was carrying a foot-ball through a Princeton rush line, or kicking a goal,—or what? His prancing step, she intimated, was perhaps better adapted to the "gridiron" than the drawing-room floor. "There is less of a *crash*,—in falling," she said. Dwarf admitted that he believed his cousin guilty of a pun.

"Since then," he added, "I have never danced. I've sat out and yawned 'graveyards' and looked grouchy."

"Boots" Paige chronicled a passage in Sprague's life at his father's cottage at Bar Harbor the preceding summer.

"There was a musical or something," said he; "say thirty people. Dwarf was all in his glory that evening. I saw him stupidly standing in front of a girl a long time, and his index finger behind his back, beckoning to me for help. It was pathetic, but we none of us went near him. He could n't tear himself away from that girl. He kept up his signals, and he hardly spoke a word to the girl but 'yes' and 'no.' Finally my sister took pity and went to his relief. The goat said, in his agitation, 'Thank you so much!' and the girl cut him dead the rest of the evening."

The rest laughed.

"That's right," acknowledged Sprague. "She asked me about 'boating,' and I had n't a word to say."

"Of course not. Oh, inexperienced member of two winning crews——"

"Ah, but she asked me if I would n't see—er —that the crews wore coats in future when in a race."

"That's a different matter."

"It gave me a blue funk," said Sprague, uneasily. "I felt like sinking through the floor, you know."

Tad Nelson said his two sisters were coming on and going to make a plunge at the Prom., and he would coach them not to speak of athletics. "You'd like my sister Kate, Dwarf."

"Would I?" asked Sprague, vaguely.

"She's not pretty, but she's nice."

"Oh," said Sprague, "I'm glad she's nice. Sorry I'm not going to be on hand."

"Why not?"

"Oh, too busy."

"See here, Dwarf, Kate has asked particularly to meet you. She saw your picture in a New York paper last year. Now, old man, I don't want to disappoint her. I said you would be at the Prom., and when I promise poor little Kate anything it's got to go, see? She was ill nearly all last winter, and she was made ill by rescuing a child from drowning on the ice—I should say a break in the ice—on the river at Yonkers. She isn't at all pretty, and she's small; and she won't make you talk, and I'll coach her about boating; and really, old man, I don't want to disappoint her, you know."

Dwarf Sprague moved uneasily in his chair and swallowed his coffee.

"Tell me about that affair," said he. "She pulled a child out of the water, did she? How big a child?"

This was not what the Dwarf probably meant to ask, but he was interested. *That* was something, and Tad Nelson followed up his advantage.

"Oh, a little boy, I believe—a little fool of a boy. She was skating, and there were plenty of men about, they said, but she was the only one who dared go on the cracking ice; and she held the child's head out of water, and got into the water herself and got chilled, and then they got planks and brought them both ashore. We all thought it awfully brave of her—a mere little girl, you know—but she herself, she made light of it."

Sprague did n't say anything. Boots Paige winked at Tad. The latter winked back. The Dwarf rose after a minute or two and went into another room, ostensibly to read what *Harper's Weekly's* bland young man had to say that week about college athletics. Presently he wandered back and took Nelson aside.

"I say, Tad, she held the child's head up, did she, and those damned, pusillanimous, contemptible cads, I suppose, they just watched her, eh?—just watched her? Stood on the bank, I dare say—got into a damned safe place, I dare say, eh?—and watched a girl—a little girl, too—watched her save the kid's life!" He was red with rage.

Sprague, who had probably saved a dozen or so, first and last, from drowning, at various times and places,—he was a noted swimmer,—

seemed to feel the ignominiousness of the behavior of his fellow-men very keenly.

"And—she wants you to dance with her at the Prom.," said Nelson.

"Tad!—I can't dance; but, I say, I—I don't want to disappoint that little girl. Not pretty,—small, and nice, you said. Can she hold her tongue, Tad? Can she keep her head up, and sit up well, and wait for orders, I mean, of course,—ha—ha—you know. And she's been ill! I say, it's a damned outrage that any dastardly man could let her do what he did!"

"I want her to have a good time, and as she's set her heart on seeing you there——"

"I suppose seeing me somewhere else—say at your room—would n't do? Give a tea, old man. How would that do?"

"No. That won't do. You 've got to do this thing for my sake, Dwarf. She will tell you herself——"

"I was n't going."

"But you will, now?" asked Tad, earnestly.

Dwarf hesitated a moment. "Well, yes, just for your sake, Tad;—and *hers*. I—I like to think of that little girl."

Tad Nelson went back to his friends with a broad grin and Sprague left the club.

"That was clever of you, Tad," drawled Lazy Aldrich, puffing out a cloud of smoke. "What the deuce will you do when he discovers the ruse?—and offers to thrash you for lying?"

"Well, my sisters *are* coming on," laughed Tad.

"Coach one of them to tell the same tale about the life-saving act——"

"Better say nothing," said Boots. "It will confuse Dwarf more. More fun for us,—see. It will be immense to see him perform——"

"He might bolt. But, fellows, I think as I made him promise to be on hand, the cold 'bot' is on you."

And it was Sunday afternoon too!!

I will not attempt to describe "Prom." week at New Haven. I will not describe the class germans, the receptions, the jolly little suppers in jolly little college rooms; I will not even make a "bluff," as they say, at the ball itself. "It's a great week for the girls!" as Barney, the hackman, has often said, and they flock into town with their pretty fluffy wings, and their amusing little "Oh, how I wish I were a man!" And they look down from the chapel gallery, and they are found in the library, and they are seen on the crosswalks, and they explore the "gym.," and they have such a good time, and they never are tired, and they perch on your window seat, and they try on your boxing-gloves, and they try your foils, and they turn their backs on your photographs of ballet dancers, and they ask *when* you study, and they say they "know" Latin, and they talk of new books, and they *so* admire Trilby, and they ask is n't Gibson in *Life* just splendid! And *then* they sigh and say again, "Heigho! I wish I were a man!"

And from the looks of things at the end of this remarkable century they will soon get their wish!

Perhaps the sedate Smith, known as a "greasy grind," has no such pleasant experience of Prom. week. His mother and sister *may* visit him. If so, they don't "visit" the Prom. Life to them is too earnest, serious, and hard for gaiety, for dances, for fun. Plain Elizabeth Smith, with sad eyes, wanders about the yard with her grouchy brother, and they discuss poor Uncle Henry's lunacy, or Cousin Emma's foolish marriage, or sister Charlotte's high stand at Mt. Holyoke, and the prospect of poor Smith's getting something to do just as soon as he graduates. Not very jolly, but dead *earnest!*—which is much better!

Prom. week came that year with a furious blizzard-like storm, but the pretty queens braved it, pneumonia, grip, and all, and appeared in such array and with such a fusillade of eyes at the ball itself, that the students yielded at once, without a second fire.

Ah me, they have "yielded" this way for twenty years!

Tad Nelson arrived a little late with his mother and sisters. The floor was swinging under Lander's conception of a Walteufel waltz, which was to be followed by a Sousa two-step. How perfectly glorious it was! The blood tingled in one's veins at the sound. Even Sprague, fired by the music, nervously pranced and charged back and forth near the entrance, waiting for the ladies to arrive. How much he would have given *then* to have learned in Freshman year the "light fantastic." Somebody's words to Cromwell kept hurrying through his mind. "Ah, Dwarf, hadst thou but learned to dance in Freshman year, as well as thou hast to row, the girls and their cards would not have deserted thee at this, thy hour of trial!" In his agitation, expectancy, and regret, he struck his two huge hands together, and his lavender gloves split across the palms and on the back from little finger to thumb, and just then, lo! Tad and the ladies appeared!

Of course, there was nothing to do but to thrust his hands behind his back, under the tails of his coat, and keep them there!

Coming down in the carriage, Tad had said, casually: "Oh, by the by, Capt. Sprague, of the crew—awfully good, honest fellow—remember, girls, be sweet to him. He's one of my best friends. There is one thing I want to impress upon you, if he offers to shake hands —*don't!* He will forget and crush your rings into your fingers—he has a terrible grip—strongest man in College, you know. Then, whatever he says, *don't deny it.* Let him have his say out."

"Well, he must be a sort of Sandow," said Kate. "I don't think I shall like him——"

"A most remarkable sort of a young man, indeed!" exclaimed his mother.

"Just let him say what he pleases. Possibly, Kate, he'll give you some sort of a bluff about your being known to him by repute—he'll pretend to have read about you in the papers, to have heard you 've done some brave act, or have taken a prize at school—or *something!* Don't dispute him; it's his little joke—agree with him, or—or he may insist on shaking hands. . . . Ah, here we are!"

"I 'm sure I shall be frightened to death at him!" said Nell, a tall, pretty blonde.

"And I—I hope I can avoid him—but I see his name down on my card—oh, Tad! six—seven times!" exclaimed Kate, a tall, pretty brunette.

"Many a girl is eating her heart out to-night, just to have a look at him! Captain of the 'Varsity crew—think of it!" and Tad Nelson prayed for forgiveness beneath his thin but growing moustache. As he got out and opened the carriage door at the entrance to the Armory, he said again, "Mind, now—don't shake his hand."

"I think we 'd better shake *him*, from what

you say," laughed Kate, merrily, getting out. "Tho', dear Tad, I would n't hurt *your* feelings for the world!"

Almost the first man they saw on the way to the dressing-room was the Dwarf, hurrying to and fro, like a mad animal in his cage, his hands hid behind his back. Tad presented him—he did not offer to shake, and he seemed to look from Kate to Nell, and back again to Kate, as if trying to see in one of them that "plain, nice little girl" Tad had told him about, "who had saved the life of that little fool of a boy." Both were tall, healthy-looking young girls, and were dressed in most becoming gowns, with enormous fluffy shoulders. Sprague, greatly embarrassed, not knowing anything better to do, at last offered his arm to Kate, who had thrown back her opera cloak, and bolted with her just as she was onto the ballroom floor.

Mrs. Nelson put up her lorgnette in astonishment. Tad was convulsed with laughter.

"What sort of a man *can* he be?" she gasped. "*Really*,—Tad!"

"Oh, it's only his way, mamma. He has such a *taking* way, you see!"

"But, pray, what will he do with her?"

"I have not the slightest idea!"

"Mamma,—he was dreadfully embarrassed,—that was all," said Nelly. "To my mind, it all looks very disagreeably like one of Tad's *infamous* practical jokes."

They hurried to the dressing-room and disposed of their wraps. When they came down, Tad presented Mr. Paige, and Mr. Aldrich, and Mr. Horner, and Mr. Barrington, and Mr. Raymond, and Mr. Gardiner, a number of his distinguished classmates, whose names were already inscribed on his sister's dance-cards. They entered the floor to the time of one of Sousa's spirited two-steps. Nellie was speedily wafted away in the respectful arms of Boots Paige. They looked anxiously and in vain for Kate, and Tad was dispatched to find her.

The "push" was very great, and the "queens" were out, of course, in most dazzling and overwhelming numbers. Tad Nelson edged his way around to the left of the vast ballroom of bunting and evergreen and flowers, bowing to this one, dropping one of his very original compliments in the ear of a blue-eyed beauty:

"How well you are looking this evening, Miss Mary!"

Soon as he came upon Dixwell and Whately, two members of the floor committee, who seemed to be laughing over some little private joke of their own, he asked anxiously:

"Have you seen Sprague and my sister?"

"Was it *your* sister?"

"Why,—what——"

"Oh, nothing—Dwarf tried to dance the end of the waltz, and slipped and fell down,—that's all; think he tore a hole in your sister's dress, —and—she's over there in the corner forgiving him, I suppose; at least, he's on his knees,— and we've had a lot of fun already out of him!"

Tad looked. Dwarf certainly was on his knees over the torn lace on Kate's skirt. He caught Kate's imploring glance and hastened to her.

"Well!" he exclaimed.

"Come here!" cried Kate, half in anger, half laughing, and he leaned down his head. "Do take this crazy Mr. Sprague out somewhere, and—let him cool down a little in the snow, and return to a glimmering of reason. Do you know what he says? He's been thinking about me for six whole days,—and that he knows all about my rescuing some bad little boy at Yonkers,—and he wishes *he'd* been there,—and that if *I am* plain, I'm nice,—and the kind of girl he likes, and that he has been thinking and thinking and thinking about me!"

Tad looked at Sprague, who had risen now, his hair dishevelled, his lavender gloves in ruin, his face bathed in perspiration,—and his heart misgave him. Poor, dear old Dwarf!

"I think, Mr. Sprague," said Kate, laughing, much relieved to take the arm of her brother, "that you have quite mistaken the person you were talking to."

"Isn't this Kate,—your nice little sister, Tad? Great heavens! Have I made a mistake?"

"This is my *cousin*, Dwarf. My sister could not come. If you had not been so precipitate, Dwarf, you might have—er—er—known it yourself!"

Then Sprague in the handsomest manner, showing what a thorough gentleman,—what a noble-hearted, clumsy, ignorant old fellow he was, said:

"I ask your pardon, Miss Nelson. I am very sorry,—I apologize for saying what I did. You are not at all plain, Miss Nelson; you are not even little. I should have known,—but I'm so fond of Tad,—that I promised to come to the Prom. just to see his nice little sister Kate, and to try and make his nice little sister have the best time I could. I am mortally sorry——"

He looked so big, so true, so handsome, with that fine waterman's bronze of his, which even the thaws and freezings of January cannot quite wear off, that Kate, eyeing him a moment, said disappointedly, with a slight quivering of the lip:

"Indeed, Mr. Sprague,—but I *am* that 'nice' little sister Kate!"

Dwarf looked blankly at Tad. The latter tried to laugh, failed, dropped Kate's hand from his arm.

"Was there ever believing any girl!" he cried, pretending great irritation, and marched off, leaving them together again.

"But you are not plain,—really!" insisted Sprague, earnestly. "You,—you are really the prettiest girl at the Prom.!"

"I believe you!" she laughed, convulsed.

"And are you really—Tad's sister or his cousin?"

"His sister—Yes." She gazed at him with truthful gray eyes.

"And you never saved the little kid through the ice?"

"No; that's a myth."

"A horse? One of Tad's stories?"

"Yes." (Laughter, and a long pause.)

"I—I—think I like you,—er—just the same,—as before—just as if you *had* saved that little chap."

"Why?"

"Because,—er—um—I never met a girl before,—er—who broke the ice so—so easily for a fellow,—it's really no work to talk to you, really!"

"Oh, Mr. Sprague! You are such a flatterer! It was *you* who broke the ice!"

"Oh, but I mean it. Before most girls I,—I—am dumb."

"But you are wofully inconstant. You'd got your mind made up evidently to a dumpy little plain girl,—and—and—look up at me!"

"By Jove!—you would n't have me constant

to a fake girl, would you? There is no nice little plain sister,—ergo,—you will have to do!"

"And be number two?"

"No, number one."

"But, I'm *sure* I cannot hope to fill that nice, dumpy little creature's place. Describe her, Mr. Sprague? Did she waddle as she walked,—a sort of a duck of a girl? Tell me— the girl you were ever thinking—thinking— thinking of!" Then she burst out again into almost a shriek of laughter.

He gave her his arm, and they strolled across the floor, in animated half-confidential conversation now. Boots Paige and Aldrich looked at him in perfect amazement. He'd never been known to say three words to a girl before in his life. Kate pulled him through a lancers, and then danced a waltz with Paige.

"Oh, he's one of the dearest,—most unselfish fellows in the world," said Paige in her ear as they whirled to the Strauss waltz; "and were it only not for the fact——"

"What, Mr. Paige?"

"I really hate to say—captain of the crew too——"

"Is it anything dreadful, Mr. Paige?"

(Solemnly.) "Well, he has—a wooden leg."

"Poor man; *that's* why he fell with me!"

"He lost it honorably,—for him."

"How? Do tell me, Mr. Paige!"

Lander's band in the gallery came out with a blare of trumpets—the music was fine!—he shouted:

"In a saw-mill——"

"Oh, how shocking!"

"He fell asleep on a log,—he has a way of sleeping just like a log,—and the polite proprietor of the saw-mill did not like to disturb him;—and when he saw he'd cut off one leg, —he said: 'there's no use taking two bites of this cherry,—why not cut off both at once?'"

Kate pretended to look horrified, but as she was waltzing, no one thought otherwise than that Paige might have trod, by accident, on her slipper.

"But the funny thing of it was, he's something of an oarsman and Harvard protested the wooden leg as extra machinery and he had to tow it behind the whole four miles."

"Mr. Paige!"

"Yes."

"Do you think I believe all that? Do you wish to make me *like* Mr. Sprague? Let me tell you there is nothing so fascinating to me as *his* sincerity."

They stopped dancing and she pointed to two harp-like set "pieces" at the end of the gallery:

"Are those emblems of the Junior Class?" she asked demurely.

"They look like harps," said Paige. "They seem rather faded——"

"They look to me like——"

"Say it—oh, say it. I suppose you mean 'blasted lyres!'"

Paige turned Miss Kate over to Aldrich for a two-step, without another word.

"Don't you think Mr. Sprague jolly?" Aldrich asked as they danced, still working the joke which had been passed along.

"Well, I would hardly say jolly. Earnest is better. And I like him—he's sincere."

"Such a pity he inherits his father's fatal disease."

"Oh, does he? He looks so strong——"

"They say he'll die of it."

"Indeed!"

"His father was the first gentleman to be hanged in Montana; quite an honor, was n't it?"

"I should say."

"He 'll be hanged as his father was—really now—on the level——"

"And be skied, afterwards, because he seems really good!"

"That 's right! He is good. Ah there, Barrington? You want the 'last half.' You can't have it Barry, can he, Miss Nelson?"

"N—yes, if he wants it. I want to hear a new little fiction about the only honest and truthful man in your class."

They had stopped dancing.

"Am I so untruthful?" asked Paige, looking admiration in his eyes.

"You are Ananias's third cousin, at *least*," she laughed.

Barrington, with a heavy basso profundo voice, asked Miss Kate, as they commenced to dance:

"You are a Vassar Grad.?"

"No."

"Why, then, where did you learn wrestling?" He looked surprised.

"Mamma——" she hesitated. She enjoyed the fun.

"Saw you take a very pretty fall—er—out of the strongest man we have here," said Barry, seriously.

"Mr. Sprague?"

"Yes, saw you drop him very neatly."

"I'd like the credit of it, of course, for I believe in athletics, but the fact was——"

"I know—er—he'd been drinking, I suppose, quite jagged! Ah, I know it. Poor Sprague! I suppose the excitement of the Prom., and all. Odd that a man of his magnificent strength shows such a miserable weakness."

"That might account for him—a little——"

"How so?"

"*In vino veritas.* He was very truthful, Mr. Barrington, and I like truthful people."

"Yes, he was not himself!"

"He did not try to deceive me."

"No. You are too old a hand——"

"Mr. Barrington!!"

They almost stopped dancing. But they resumed as he said:

"I mean you recognized—from long and ardent mission work among the slums—you knew—er—a harmless inebriate when you saw him."

"Mr. Sprague is in training—he can't, he must n't drink——"

"Save on the sly."

"How unkind you are to him!"

"When sober, he's the dearest fellow in the world. Ah me, it's a pity he *will* imbibe the 'rosy'!"

"You positively slander him!" She drew herself up, indignantly.

"Oh, ask him, that's all—we'll ask him to drink a glass of champagne. Here he is!"

"They stopped dancing. The Dwarf was hovering near at hand, watching them.

"Mr. Sprague, will you come with us?" she asked.

"Where?" he replied, vaguely.

"And have some wine, old man?" said Barrington.

Sprague gave him a look of indignant scorn.

"Oh, you can have gin, of course," laughed Barrington; "some people prefer it—but——"

"I'm so thirsty," exclaimed Kate. "Come, Mr. Sprague."

They went into the brilliant supper-room,

which happened to be near at hand, and sat down in an obscure corner at a little table. The Juniors were doing the affair in the handsomest possible manner, and the spread was sent up from New York by a fashionable caterer. Barrington ordered a bottle of fizz, and the apoplectic French waiter disappeared and shortly appeared again with a bottle wrapped in a napkin.

"Three glasses, waiter," said Barrington.

"Not for me, of course," said the Dwarf.

The waiter poured out the wine in three glasses.

Kate Nelson looking perfectly stunning, and a very laughing devil in her eye, held up her glass, sparkling with the champagne.

"You won't refuse to drink with me, Mr. Sprague?"

"Really—you see I've begun training," he said, excusing himself.

"But the race is six months away,—if you won't drink, I shall be mortally offended."

"Mortally offended?" he repeated vaguely.

Poor Sprague! He looked at the girl, then looked at Barrington, who enjoyed his dilemma; then he looked at the girl again.

"I'm captain this year, Miss Kate,—and—and—the example,—really, you know——"

"Then if no one sees you,—and it's on the sly?"

"No, by Jove! (half laughing). Of course I'll not do on the sly what I won't do openly." Then he rose, flushed, and getting provoked.

"Gad!" said Barrington, recounting the incident afterward; "he looked deuced handsome too.

"'Drink,—please—just one little swallow!' Her eyes pleaded. She acted as though she really was bound, womanlike, to make him yield, if she could. 'One swallow,' she laughed and teased him, 'does not make a summer!'

"She stood up too," said Barrington, "and if any girl *looked* volumes at a fellow, I swear she did at Dwarf Sprague. Her dark eyes seemed to be full of chain lightning. You know what a beauty she is!

"'Will you not?' they seemed to say. 'Then choose between Yale and me!'

"'No! I will not!' his eyes answered, defiantly.

"Oh, the Capt. has got quite a grit in his way!" added Barrington.

"'You care more for Yale than anything in this world,' she said. 'And—I quite think you're right.'

"Then I was surprised to see Miss Kitty Nelson laugh and toss her upraised glass of very good Pommery on the floor, and take the Dwarf's arm and walk off with him, at the same time giving *me* the haughtiest, most supercilious and disdainful glance I ever got from a woman or man, over her shoulder as she went away. She made me feel like a villain!

"Well,—I was left alone to finish the fizz, and pay for broken glass,—and—and that possibly accounts for my losing my dance-card, and not seeing Miss Kate again during the entire evening!"

"I noticed that you had quite a 'still' on afterwards that evening," said Aldrich, laughing, "and yet you looked quite glum too."

"I think if the Dwarf had not got the start of me—I——"

"Oho—I see!" said Aldrich, compassionately. Then Aldrich began to whistle absent mindedly:

"Oh, my love is a Bowery girl."

Boots Paige, Barrington, Aldrich, and others congratulated Tad Nelson when they met a few days later. "The Dwarf's governor is ten times a millionaire out in Ohio," they said; "and, well,—he's admittedly one of the *few* honest men in the class!"

"Oh,—it could n't suit *me* better," said Tad, who now complacently played the heavy indulgent father to his sister and her *fiancé;* "I planned it all out from the start. I persuaded him to go, you know; and I got him interested. They are just suited. Just suited."

"Let's go over and shake the honest old Dwarf's hand off!" said Aldrich.

And they tried to,—but could n't!

THE LAST CRUISE OF THE "NANCY BRIG."

"I 'm a bose'n tight, and a midshipmite,
And the crew of the *Nancy Brig*."

IT was a mild, sunny April day, one of those mild warm days of early spring, which, such is our eventful climate, give the weatherwise cause to expect " storms with varying winds— and rain," but which only bring to the student-mind visions of June, and recollections of the last summer, and make them, to a man, foolishly leave off winter underclothing.

The Campus, this mild April morning, was making an effort in spots to put forth a blade of green grass. Not a green thing visible but Freshmen—was no longer to be the order of things that year. The crew of the *Nancy* decided that it was just the day to go " down the harbor."

The *Nancy Brig*, as the six owners rechristened her from the *Swallow*, was a cat-boat some twenty-eight feet long and proportionately wide and shallow, with a centre-board that went down into the depths of the sea and dragged up innocent young oysters from their beds; a mast which towered into the clouds, and had the class numerals, "Umpty-three," on a white pennant floating at its head; a well setting sail, a rakish overhang. The *Nancy* had been known to give one or two fast sharpies a hard tussel out of New Haven harbor. She had been tied up until within a few days, when "Tad" Nelson, and Paige and Barrington, spent an entire Saturday afternoon and, I grieve to say, part of Sunday putting her into commission for the season.

They gave her hull a new coat of white paint, and daubed her inside dark blue, out of patriotic feeling. Then they sailed her around to the flats, just off the N. H. Yacht Club house, dropped anchor in the mud, and she was ready and fit for anything, they said.

They had bought her, new, in Freshman year, and she had gone through with them to their last year in college, requiring but one renewal of sail and mast. They had had many a moonlight sail in her; they had flirted and made love in her; they had fished in her; shot in her; crammed for annuals in her,—lived in her a large part of the summer term.

"Sleuth" Davidson was an original owner, but they had led him astray into base-ball, and he now covered first base. "Dwarf" Sprague had been an original owner, but he had wandered off into the University crew. There were many other and finer yachts and cat-boats belonging to students, but there was none that had so many stories connected with her as the *Nancy*. She had had her turns at bad luck, too, but she had never drowned any one; among other adventures being herself run down by the night boat for New York, one night when Barrington fell asleep at the rudder. Cruising for duck the previous fall among the Thimbles, she nearly got her back broken on a sunken rock, but the tide lifted her, and she sailed home half full of sea water, safe and sound.

Well, that warm April day happened to be a Wednesday, and Tad Nelson, Paige, Phil Gardiner, "Great" Barrington, "Jack" Horner, and Keith hurried down to the boat after noon recitation, carrying with them a basket of lunch, and getting some bottles of beer at Gus

Traeger's on their way. The owners would take the first sail of the season, and it really seemed as if summer had come again.

"Do you remember the night when Sam Flemming put in his great saving act off the *Nancy?* said "Little Jack," as they jolted along down in the horse-car.

Paige remembered it with a laugh. The others had a dim recollection of hearing the story. They had not been present.

"We had taken out a party of girls that night," said Little Jack, " and we got in rather late, owing to a calm. The chaperon was anxious to get the girls home, and we hurried things along as best we could."

"I know the way *you* generally hurry things along on such occasions!" laughed Paige.

"There was a Miss Friese there from Boston. She was nice easy people. I think you 'd call her a regular queen. She was too airy fairy for me though. She could hardly open her mouth without spouting poetry. Sam Flemming was very much gone on a Miss Carrie Hathaway, and she was engaged, at the time, in putting up a sort of bluff act on him—he trying to show her he did n't give a cent for any one else,

and trying to be devoted, and she accusing *him*,
—pretending to,—as girls have a little way of
doing, confound 'em!—of only trying to give
her the grand laugh. Carrie was a regular
dazzler then, and she is now, only she's sobered down, and takes serious views of life, I
believe, since she and Flem. have made it up."

"Well, the *Nancy* got in at last on the flats,
and we dropped our anchor, and as she was getting into the rowboat Miss Friese fell overboard.
It was Sam Flemming's fault somehow, and,
without a thought, he threw off his hat and
dove overboard after her."

'It was bright moonlight and clear as day.
Flem. dove, and he must have dived hard!—it
wasn't more than two feet deep, and Flem. did
most of his diving into thick, oozy mud. His
legs stuck up in the air out of the water at first,
and then they slowly fell over on one side, and
Flem. rose up out of the mire a sight to behold. He looked like the old man of the sea,
with gory, slimy locks hanging down his back
and sides. What a sight he was! He came
up gasping, and Miss Friese, who got herself
right side up with care without much effort, in
her fright, gave a great scream, and threw her

arms around Flem.'s neck and clung to him and kissed him,—called him her Hero—her Brave Darling,—ha! ha! ha! etc. Well,—you had better believe that Miss Carrie liked *that*, and it was a long time afterward before Flem. could bring her round. But I shall never, as long as I live, forget Sam Flemming's famous dive!"

"His legs stuck out of the water half a minute!" laughed Paige, "and when he had floundered up,—it sounded so silly in Miss Friese to go on in such tremendous heroics, and clasp him to her as they stood there knee-deep in mud, as Pauline clasps Claude Melnotte in *The Lady of Lyons*. Oh, it was great! And the funny part of it was that Miss Friese took it all in perfect seriousness, and half the girls on the boat did too, and they thought Sam a hero!"

"The tides are desavin'," laughed Barrington. "I remember getting a load of people aboard the *Nancy*, hoisting sail, and then finding the centreboard buried in three feet of mud!"

"What did you do then, Great?"

"Oh, I pretended the wind was n't right, and that I had to wait for a man from shore.

The Last Cruise of the "Nancy Brig." 127

The tide rose after a little while, and I got her off."

They reached the N. H. Yacht Club house by this time, and without delay got aboard the *Nancy Brig*.

" She never looked better in her life ! " said Boots Paige.

" She 's a hummer,—an angel,—a darling, —dear old *Nancy B. !* "-cried Little Jack, delighted to have it warm and pleasant again for sailing.

" Haul away your throat halyards !—Now the peak.—Slack off your sheet there, Boots !—Lay her head a little more to starboard !—*Now* you have her ! " So sang Great Barrington, skipper.

The wind was rather light, but the tide was going out, and they hoisted sail and swung down past an anchored fishing schooner with some of the *Nancy's* old-time speed. They passed Indian Hill, now crowned with a fort, and across the stern the ruins of old Fort Hale, of '73. Now they steer across to the white, unused old lighthouse, and tack briskly out into the Sound.

" Say, boys,—ye must expect a nor'-wester

to-night," sang out an old salt from a puffing tug.

"Right, Cap!" sung out Boots in answer. He was steering the boat. What did the brave *Nancy* care for nor'-westers?

It was so warm and sunny,—what wind there was being directly with them, that they let out the sail, threw off their coats, "hit" their pipes, and prepared to enjoy life with an equal mind.

"Do you remember the story of Adams," said Phil, "and Thomas and a lot of those fellows in ' umpty-four,—in their Freshman year, who were out in the Sound in a cat, and were run down by a Fall River boat, and were picked up and carried to Newport, and for a joke hid away three days and never let any one know, and it got into all the papers,—and the Faculty offered $25 reward for their bodies?"

"Yes, it was all they were worth too!—they were a fresh set of chumps to do such a thing."

"Yes,—a regular Freshman horse!"

"There's an old story of a Yale student in 1861, who sailed over to Long Island and who left his boat keel up on the sand and his hat floating on the water and went abroad, and they never knew where he was———"

WELCH HALL.

The Last Cruise of the "Nancy Brig." 129

"Till the war was over!" suggested Tad Nelson.

"No Yale man ever avoided the draft,—no,—he owed a lot of money——"

"So—do—I," came in chorus.

"And he went over as purser on a steamer and then—got in with Maximillian,—went to Mexico with him,—and was shot there. He was in '66."

"Quite a romance," said Little Jack, musing over his pipe. "Wonder if it's true? he sang:

> "Does it seem so to you?
> Seems to me he's lyin'——
> Oh, I wonder if it's true?"

They had got well down the harbor by this time, and it was voted to run out the east channel and so on toward Brandford Point and the ever beautiful Thimble Islands, which they presently saw twinkling and gleaming in the sun to the eastward.

"The wind freshened a little and the *Nancy* made good time. Several of the fellows put on their coats.

"They say there are three hundred and sixty-five Thimbles,—one for every day in the year," said Phil Gardiner, standing up and using a marine glass. "But I can only see three from here."

"Give me the glass, old four eyes!"

A pleasant allusion to Phil's eye-glasses, by Barrington.

"I say, fellows,—perhaps we'd better not try the Thimbles," said Little Jack dubiously.

"What—with *this* wind?" and he was instantly cried down.

So they sailed, borne on the western breeze, which grew fresher as they got away from shore, and they ate lunch and drank their bottled beer with the eager joy of sailors no longer to be housed ashore.

The glistening Thimbles grew to be bits of green, then bits of brown and green, then took on definite shape. They lay like pretty floating gardens on the blue water. Paige pointed the boat well down toward Pot Rock and the cove. Here, a hundred years ago, the famous Captain Kidd, pirate and buccaneer, hid his vessel behind the rocky islands, and buried his treasure where he and no one else has since been able to find it. Only his celebrated punch-bowl, and initials remain to recall his sojourn in these charming waters.

"Hard up your helm there! Let go the sheet!" and so they came round to the little steam-boat dock.

They had run in near Kidd's punch-bowl island. As it was then three o'clock, and the wind was rising, they thought best to merely load in (unromantically) a few bottles of beer, and a pound or so of crackers, and set out for home, as soon as possible.

"Jupiter! how black those clouds are on the western horizon!" said Barrington, as they cleared the island, and made for open sea.

"Yes,—they are," chorus.

"Do you remember the skipper's telling us to look out for a nor'wester?"

"Yes,—we do," chorus.

"And the wind dead ahead too!"

The first tack was out to sea, and the waves had risen with the wind, and the great rollers, which had started somewhere down near New York, came heaving up from the westward, and suggested, with the spray that began to fly, that it would be a most excellent thing to reef.

The sail was lowered, and all hands fell to

work. She was reefed in a jiffy, but a wave pounded over her stern, and made things nasty. Little Jack fell to work bailing with a sponge and dipper. Then they hoisted the sail again and were off like a throughbred.

The wind freshened, and whatever the *Nancy* was, she was not a wind-jammer. She fell off a good deal, and they soon got pretty well away from land. It got to be five o'clock, and the heavy clouds from the west made it *seem* much later. The wind blew cold, and they shivered, and joked, and chattered, and inwardly wished they were well ashore,—inwardly, not outwardly. Barrington held the tiller with a stern, set face,—perhaps he knew the dangers of a fluffy nor'wester better than the rest, for in summer he sailed nearly every day of his life. Every now and then he cried: "Ease her off!" as the wind blew a cat's-paw. They tacked and stood in-shore. Every one was silent now, and anxious too, for the wind blew so fresh that they began to worry about the sheet, which had not been renewed since the previous summer. The halyards, Paige thought, were all right. He'd been up the mast with them and they were a good thing, he said.

The sail itself was good for a hurricane, he said; then he added, " D—n April sailing, anyhow!"

"To-day was a regular April fool day, was n't it?" said Jack Horner, cheerfully.

"No day to be out!" growled shivering Keith. "Too wet."

Then came the "I told you so's," as a wave struck the bow, and fizz—boom!—the spray covered them and drenched them to the bone; again and again the water flew over them and ran in rivulets down about the creaking centre-board.

They then took turns bailing until they were tired and back-weary. Darkness came down without the moon they had counted on. A huge mass of cloud swept ominously across the face of the sky, and Barrington, who took full command, issued his orders as short, as sharp, as fiercely as a captain's in an engagement. Two men manned the sheet and left him free to steer. Then, as the boat lurched off, in the heavy seas, Great ordered another reef.

Then came a fine stinging sleet on the wind, driving into their faces and cutting like a knife.

The reefing was done laboriously; for their

fingers were stiff with cold now; fearfully, for the waves shook the boat as the wind shakes an aspen of a summer night.

When double-reefed she rode better, and if the wind had not freshened, they might have weathered the gale; but as deep night came on, they were blown out farther and farther from shore, and were, at eight o'clock, nearly in the middle of the Sound. It was dark and they had no compass. Barrington was almost determined to let her drive before the wind.

But now a new danger appeared. After having been laid up so long all winter, the *Nancy* was "dry," and began to show it, in the banging and tossing she got, by leaking badly. She had iron ballast along her keel and enough, they knew, to send her to the oysters in no time. They worked ankle,—then knee-deep in the icy April water, and Barrington, with his set white face, was driving her before the wind to the Long Island shore; not a word of discouragement, or doubt, or misgiving had been spoken. As far as anything was *said*, they were out on a summer night's sail! The water kept gaining, and she rolled heavily and like a bilged log. Every one baled with their hats now, but it did little good. Far away in the eastward rose up two lights out of the sea. A new, sudden terror of being run down came over them.

Then, for the first time, Paige spoke up. He was holding the sheet:

"What in h—l are you doing, Great?"

"Let me alone, damn you! I know what I'm about!"

"She'll run you down!"

"Let me alone!"

"She's a tow barge—I see red and green lights—why, even she's unable to manage herself in this wind."

"Hell! I don't care; don't you see we'll all be in the water in five minutes? The tow is our only chance!" he said hoarsely. "We *may* reach it. *Let her drive!*"

Then there was a deep silence, and to nearly all there, the bright red and green lights of the tow steamer meant hope, for they were young and could not look death in the face; and it was plain they could not keep afloat many minutes longer. The waves dashed over the boat at will,—how madly, wildly, they fought to drown the lads! Piling one over the other like yelling wolves, snarling, roaring, hissing, drowning the sodden boat. Yet the lights, green and red and white, drew near, nearer,— then . . . !

. The *Nancy* swung down the wind, and then, as a water-logged boat will do in a heavy sea, sidled against the long tow hawser and her mast slipped along with a rushing swist and a bing, until she smashed against the bow of the tow, and for a brief minute hung there, held by the suction of the sea and the leaping waves. The great sail caught for a moment, then burst into a hundred flapping streamers.

Just for a minute! She hung pinned by the wind and the sea against the flat wide bow of the scow!

All scrambled up the side, helping each other on the tow in mad haste,—all but one. Great Barrington had either been hit or stunned or had fainted when she struck, and lay across the tiller as if dead.

"Great is killed!" cried Little Jack about to go down again. They seized him and held him back.

"Oh, I'll fetch him,—it's a faint!" said Boots Paige; and then, as if it were nothing, he went down again on the sinking *Nancy*, and, groping his way, bore his friend up in his arms. It was a dreadful moment!

"Just in time, old man!" they said to him, as they swiftly pulled Great up, and gave a hand to Paige. As he stepped on the deck of the scow, the *Nancy Brig*, giving a sort of mournful sob of despair, as if alive, sank out of sight,—foundered in mid-Sound, and the scow went over her.

The scow, *Ice King*, forbidding in name only, had a warm cabin, and a bottle of whiskey, and a kind-hearted skipper, and an astonished skipper's wife, and was bound for New London. Barrington, seated higher than the rest at the boat's tiller, had been struck by the boom of the *Nancy*, and knocked senseless. He revived shortly, and was not seriously hurt. Had he not shown a little sand, and steered for the tow, where would they all have been to-day?

"Why, in Davy Jones's locker," says Little Jack, with a jolly laugh. For a long time, though, you could n't get any of the "owners" to speak of that last cruise of the *Nancy Brig*. It was too deadly solemn a matter.

"Yes," said Barrington, over his pipe, "it was a close call for the 'owners.'"

"But I don't blame the dear old *Nancy!* She did her best to save, not drown us," said Little Jack, and in this opinion all concurred.

OLD SLEUTH'S LEVEL HEAD.

OLD Sleuth Davidson, the tall, good-looking, well bronzed fellow, who played first base on the 'Varsity nine last year, and never was known to lose his head on any occasion, and who always dressed (except when on the field), in the very best style (he had his clothes over from a Bond Street London tailor), and who used to spend hours over his cravat, and debate and argue for days with his chum about some unimportant matter of dress, and was always so silent and level-headed about everything else, especially about matters concerning the fairer and better sex, and who roomed in Welch, and whose stand was well up in the first division,— Well, Sleuth Davidson went off the hooks, at last, somewhat in this fashion, according to Little Jack Horner, who pumped the facts out of Sleuth's particular friend, Laze Aldrich. Little Jack afterwards went to Sleuth's dinner and got the whole story from his friends, for

Sleuth never gave himself away under any consideration, and was confoundedly mad that it got all over the class, as it did in a surprising way, long before graduation.

"You see," said Little Jack, pulling away hard at one of the Dwarf's cutty pipes, and seated with his feet on the Dwarf's study table, "you're not the only man that has been foolish enough to go and get engaged before he's out of college. Sleuth is there, too,—and I'll tell you fellows how about it.

"Sleuth was going down to New York, Thanksgiving, and he had invited his chum Paton, Aldrich, and Barrington with him for the game, and over Thanksgiving Day, at his house. He had his dress-suit case and his hat-box with him in the car,—Sleuth always travels like some benighted Englishman visiting this country for the first time,—and they settled themselves in the smoker for the two hours' run to New York, feeling, no doubt, very fit, and were exceeding glad to get away for the fun,—as we Elis all are, when we have given out, pretty generally, that the foot-ball team of the year consists of a dead man and ten cripples, left over from the Springfield game.

"Every one of the four fellows was trying to look his smoothest, you know, with the usual blue violets in his button-holes, and new hats and clothes and all. Sleuth had promised them a good time in New York and some very charming girls to meet,—friends of his sister. It seems she had arranged a dinner and theatre party that very night for them, and they naturally anticipated a very agreeable sort of a time, all round.

"Well, the express had run along down near to Fairfield, when Great Barrington looked out and said: 'Quick, fellows!—a stunning girl,—on horseback!' And they looked out and saw a stylish queen on a thoroughbred, on the road which crossed the track. Sleuth stuck his head out of the window to get a better look, and Gee! his new silk hat blew off,—and, what does he do, but right then and there, quick as a flash, he throws out his hat-box after the hat!

"The train was going at sixty miles an hour, and the box must have fallen a good distance from the hat, of course.

"'I suppose you were so confounded mad to lose your hat, you thought you might as well throw out your hat-box too,' laughed Barrington.

"'I never saw you lose your head before, Sleuth,' said Paton, amazed.

"'I did n't,—I only lost my hat,' said Sleuth, calmly.

"'Well, the queen was worth it! Very easy people!' said Great.

"'Sleuth,—why the devil did you make such an idiot of yourself?' asked Aldrich, laughing.

"Old Sleuth quietly fitted his smoking-cap on his head and kept very still for a few moments; then he said, in that slow, dry way he has: 'My hat-box has my address in town on it. Er—you see it's the only way I could think of to get my hat back again.—A new hat and hat-box too.'

"'You 'll never see either hat or box again,—you jack!' laughed Paton.

"'You don't know your Connecticut,' said Sleuth. 'I 'll bet I get it back to-morrow in time for the game. Some honest old hayseed farmer 'll pick it up and express it. Perhaps the fair rider herself will be kind enough to favor—'

Old Sleuth's Level Head.   143

"'What!—dismount from her horse, just for a hat? Oh, no; the track walker will wear it Sundays, Sleuth, and the box will do for his tools.'

"'Twenty even you don't see both hat and box again, Sleuth,' said Paton, thinking he had a snap.

"'Oh, very good,' drawled Sleuth. 'Make it fifty.' And he took out a wad of Harvard money he had pinched at Springfield.

"'I'll make it fifty,—you don't see both hat and box before the game to-morrow!' said Paton. 'Is it a go?'

"'I don't mind,' said Sleuth.

"'I'll place a modest ten on the same terms,' said Aldrich.

"'Count me in,—same as Laze,' echoed Barrington.

"Sleuth accommodated them all, and then they lit cigars and went to work and played whist at a dollar a corner, until they had to get out at the Forty-second Street Depot, although it was in the midst of a hand.

"They went to the Davidsons' house on Forty-seventh Street, and Sleuth borrowed a hat from his younger brother Ben, who was home from Andover and who happened to have the big head that year, from shutting out Exeter in foot-ball. The hat fitted Sleuth in great shape.

"They dressed for dinner. Sleuth's mother had invited half a dozen swagger girls, Alice's friends, to dinner, and they had a good deal of fun over Sleuth's being so fond of the sex that he'd risk his hat for seeing them. They made fun of his throwing out the hat-box too, and all went off to the theatre in a jolly frame of mind. Old Sleuth, as was his habit, kept very still, grinned, and hardly said a word."

"Just like him!" laughed several listeners, and Little Jack continued.

"Sleuth's sister, Alice,—you remember her at the Prom. last year?—a bright, spicy, snappy sort of girl, said it was dollars to doughnuts—or words to that effect—that that girl on a horse at Fairfield picked up the hat and box, and her brother would hear from it again. She and the girls all took a most romantic view of the incident, and quite worked on Sleuth's feelings, and kept him on the anxious seat with their guying.

"His brother Ben said he hadn't a doubt

the hat would come back, and then he winked the other eye! He made up a burlesque on 'The Cat Came Back,' and sang it all over the house. (I tell you, that brother Ben is going to make a great chap some of these days,— when he comes down to Yale. He's a corker for a young kid!)

"Well, after the theatre, they started out to do the town. They drove down to the Fifth Avenue Hotel, and met a lot of the fellows and got on a few shy bets with some Princeton men who wanted odds—three to one. Then they opened a bot., and got one or two other Elis in with them and started for the Bowery. But, fellows, the Bowery is n't much nowadays, —it 's very slow; they took in one or two beer halls and drove back to the Hoffman House, where there was a sort of mild riot going on, and the peelers were trying to haul a young tough to the station-house, all done up in blue ribbons and shouting he was a '*Yale Soft More.*' There were more Yale students in blue, with square, heavy jaws, bull-dog phizes, and Bowery lingo, than any Yale monitor would have owned up to! They set on to the peelers, and there was a lively rough-and-tumble scrimmage right then and there, which was fully described next day in the papers as 'a grand student spree.' I don't believe there was a single Yale or Princeton or Harvard man in it—not one!

"So they had a rarebit and a mug of ale, and all went comfortably home to Sleuth's house, and he put the two additional friends up; they slept three in a room,—there never was such a hospitable fellow as Sleuth,—and they all slept the sleep of the just and dreamed of the game and the usual victory.

"The next morning, when they came down, rather late, for breakfast, there, in the hall on the hat-stand, was Sleuth's hat-box, with an American Express label on it, and the hat inside, as fresh and new as the day he bought it!

"'The expressman just brought it in, sir,' said the servant.

"Sleuth calmly opened the box and tried on the hat, not at all surprised. 'It's been ironed,' he said. A card dropped out as Sleuth put the hat on, and Paton picked it up. It read:

> "Here's to the man who thinks it but his duty
> To lose his hat in looking at a beauty.
> Here's to the man who sees his hat return,
> And searches far 'for whom it may concern!'"

"Sleuth read it over twice—there was no other clue or address,—and drawled: 'That sounds like one of those rank mottoes you find in a German favor,—does n't it?'

"'That girl is a thoroughbred—it's an invitation!' laughed Great.

"'Odd,—that a girl would know enough to have the hat ironed!' said Sleuth, musingly, taking his hat off and looking it over.

"'Oh, you unsentimental cad!' said Paton, who, as stakeholder, turned over the money they bet to Sleuth. Of course, that girl on horseback wrote it! and she practically invites you to a Fairfield—and no favor!'

"'It's very astonishing!' mused Sleuth.

"'Why, yes,—that girl on horseback we saw,' said Aldrich, and he and Great at once 'borrowed' back their money bet and lost from good-natured Sleuth, and they went out of the house, and down to the Fifth Avenue Hotel to hunt bets, profoundly impressed with Old Sleuth's presence of mind and level head.

"'Well,—*I* never expected you'd see that hat or box again!' laughed Paton.

"'Why,—*of course!*' drawled Sleuth, disdainfully.

"The hat — Dewlap's eight-dollar tile — just as good as new, as you shall hear, my lads!" and Little Jack laughed and his merry little eyes twinkled in glee.

"Well, Thanksgiving day was bright and fair; New York was all blue and yellow, from the Battery to the Park. After a jolly lunch, they went out to the game on a coach, and on the coach ranged up alongside of theirs was one on which there was a party of yellow Princeton men, and there was on it, too, one of the girls who had been at Davidson's dinner the night before.

"On the box seat of the Princeton coach, sat a perfect stunner,—a stranger,—but by all odds the prettiest queen on the grounds. Jove! but she was a corking beauty,—raven locks and gazelle eyes, and all that sort of thing! Men turned around and stared their eyes out at her. It was an awful pity that she was done up in yellow instead of blue,—but she *was*. And she waved a great big yellow silk flag too, with a black 'P' in the centre, and was what the poets call a cynosure of all eyes." Little Jack smacked his lips over the word.

"'What do you say to that in yellow,

Sleuth?' asked Barrington, indicating the queen. 'Pretty smooth people—eh?'

"'I've kept my eye on that some time. Wait till you see me take her away from the Nassaus!' drawled Old Sleuth. 'I'm going over to meet her in a minute. There is Miss Lincoln (one of the girls who dined with them the night before), and I know two of the Princeton men—devilish good fellows.'

"Sleuth got down from the coach,—it was a good half hour before the game,—and the next thing they saw, he was talking and laughing to that queen in yellow as if he'd known her all his life.

"Gee! the Nassaus stood looking on as if knocked silly. The girl seemed to take to Sleuth in some extraordinary way, from the first. Love at first sight, I guess.

"Paton and Aldrich, on the Yale coach, shook their heads. 'Old Sleuth is a winner, again,' they said, admiringly. 'What a wonderful level head he has!'

"There he was, sitting by her side talking and monopolizing her, and the Nassaus couldn't seem to get near her. Oh, Sleuth always did love to fuss the girls. Miss Lincoln, sitting behind seemed convulsed, and kept telegraphing over to Alice Davidson, and there was some joke going on among the girls and Ben that the men could n't quite gather.

"While he was over there, the Elis sang:

> "'Don't send my boy to Princeton,
> He is my only lad, etc., etc.,'

and that made the queen laugh and wave her flag only the harder, and pretty soon the two teams came out for preliminary practice, and Sleuth trundled back to his own coach again, highly pleased with himself, and they all congratulated him. He said :—

"'Who is she? Why, she's from Fairfield,—she's the *very* girl we saw on horseback,—her name is Miss Louise Palfrey. She sent her groom to pick up my hat and box, and expressed them back to me! I said that some one would pick 'em up—I hoped the girl would —and she did!

"'When I got over there she was telling a Princeton man the incident : "First, I saw a hat fly out," said she; "and then, to my astonishment, a hat-box flew out after it. And I half expected to see a man come flying out after the box,——it was all so queer! I sent my groom for the hat and box, and expressed them at once to the owner."

"'"Not without a message," said I, repeating the poem she had sent.

"'"Oh!" she laughed, blushing, "are *you* the Mr. Davidson?"

"'"I am the man," I laughed, "and I take off the very same hat to you now!"

"'"This is almost too good to be true!" she laughed, and Miss Lincoln laughed too, very much amused, and added, in a whisper to Miss Palfrey which I overheard, "Anything to beat Yale!"

"' She's awfully smooth you know, and full of fun. It seems she and Miss Lincoln are old friends. Now, isn't it queer? and I'm sure my mother would say it was all very providential.'

"And Sleuth the goat, beamed all over with the innocent joy and the excitement of first love.

"Well, the teams lined up, the substitutes got off behind the side lines, and in a hushed silence the great game began.

"Then we gave a cheer, and the Nassaus

gave their 'Siss—Boom!' three times, and we quieted down again, and got ready to do Princeton up in great shape, but we could n't seem to make any headway. The ball was in our territory most of the time. We rooted hard, too, and did a lot of shouting and yelling, but the Nassaus tore holes through our line and played horse with us. They see-sawed all around our left end, and it was all we could do to stand 'em off the first half with neither side a goal.

"Our dandy team played a logy, tired sort of game, as if each man had been given knock-out drops, and we all felt blue!

"Then, in the intermission, Sleuth went over and talked to Miss Palfrey again, and drank champagne, and told of the great things Yale would do next half. He bet gloves and candy with her no end, just to please her. 'Why,' he said, 'we'll push 'em all over the block next half. They're not in it.'

"But when he got back to our coach he shook his head, and said the game was a sure goner,—that Princeton would surely do us up in the second half. But when the team came out, we gave 'em the long cheer all the samey!

    " Breka Co ax Co ax Co ax!
    Breka Co ax Co ax Co ax!
     O—up! O—up!
      Para Boloo
    Yale! Yale! Yale!
(Ter)   Rah, Rah, Rah,
      Yale!!

"Then the second half began and it was evident that Yale was n't in it a little bit;—Princeton got a goal in ten minutes;—then we held 'em down in a desperate bull-dog fashion till the end;—it was awful!

"I don't believe Old Sleuth really cared a continental for the game. He pretended to be terribly broken up though; and Miss Palfrey, going home on the coach, out of pity, consented to wear his bunch of blue violets. It was a 'crush,' you see, on both sides, and I wish the story ended just there, for dear Old Sleuth's sake, but it does n't.

"You see, as soon as they got back to town, there was the regular Thanksgiving dinner party, and in the midst of it Old Sleuth was called out to pay a bill. Dewlap sent up their bill for a high hat and hat-box.

"'What's this?' asked Sleuth of the man, in amazement.

"'Hat and box purchased this morning,' said the man. 'Bill to be paid to-night. Them's the orders.'

"'What! I never bought a hat this morning.'

"'H. J. Davidson; that's the name. Hat and hat-box delivered early this morning too.'

"'Why,—I thought *that* was——the one I lost on the train!' gasped Sleuth, beginning to catch on.

"'All I knows on,' said the man, 'is that the goods is new and ain't paid fer, an' I want the money—thirteen dollars.'

"Sleuth coughed up the money, and went back to the table a wiser and a silenter man than ever. But Ben and Alice guyed him half to death. Poor Old Sleuth! It was a put-up job!"

"Say,—hold on, Little Jack!" said his listeners. "You don't mean——"

"I do! It was a clean beat! Ben went down to Dewlap's early that morning and ordered a new hat for Sleuth and a new hat-box, and pasted Sleuth's card on it, and it was that he found on the hat-stand!"

"And the verses?"

"Not bad, were they? Alice and Ben made

'em up, and put up the job just to take the conceit out of their elder brother!

"But Sleuth, who never loses his head, did lose his heart. He admits he is dead crushed on that Louise Palfrey, who lives in Baltimore. But then, what does a college crush amount to anyway?"

"Poor dear Old Sleuth!" laughed the Dwarf.

"Oh, he just grinned and said nothing at all about it. He got Ben to box four rounds with soft gloves before he went back to college, and poor Ben (a plucky young chap, who will surely make his place on the Yale team some day) went back to school with a pair of lovely black eyes! Sleuth told him he was paying for that hat! I don't know what he has on hand for Alice; but Sleuth, with his long head, will get even somehow!

"But Sleuth paid his bets llke a man, and what's more, to keep the grind on the dead quiet, gave a very nice little dinner a week later at the club (I was present), and at which he intimated that 'All's well that ends well,' and that if all went as well as he had reason to expect, his engagement ring would probably cost his whole month's allowance!"

NAT HALE OF '73.

"During the Christmas holidays," said "Great" Barrington, one night, in Keith and Horner's room, in Lawrance Hall, "I was in New York——"

"Little Jack" was strumming to himself on his banjo in a corner and softly jingling:

> "There's nothing in the world goes wrong,
>   Nay, nay—nay, nay—
> There's nothing in the world goes wrong!"

"Ah, there, how was the Tenderloin? Has Dr. Parkhurst washed the Augean stables and made the city over new? What did you see? And how was dear Ada Rehan?"

This from Little Jack Horner.

"I was in New York," continued Barrington, with a serious air, "and I had an experience—with——"

"Tell us who she was,—was it Tad's sister Nelly? I hope not, because we'll have to fight, of course,—coffee and pistols, and all that." And Little Jack sang—

"And when your hair is gray or gone, quite gone,
Make merry all the same, we say—we say—we say—"

"I had an experience which made me feel that we *young* Elis don't know it all or do it all, after all," continued Barry.

"Which it goes without sayin' is a very wise ree-mark," said Little Jack, solemnly, laying aside his banjo.

"I'd been down to Newspaper Row, to the *It's So* office to see Bud Thompson of Umpty-seven, who writes some of those funny Bowery stories,—you know. I left Bud at just twelve o'clock midnight, on Friday night—Hangman's Day,—and I walked across City Hall Park towards the Sixth Avenue Elevated station at a rapid gait.

"There was no one in sight, and it was storming a little, and you can imagine I was somewhat surprised to hear a voice call out behind me, 'I say, are you a Yale man? So am I, '73.'

"I stopped and waited a moment, but could see no one, and thought I must have been entirely mistaken."

"Oh, what a jag, my boy! my boy!" laughed Paige.

"Shut up; let him tell his yarn," said the "Dwarf."

"I walked on, then heard the voice again, behind me:

"'I say,—hold on, there! How are things up at New Haven? Give us the news.'

"I stopped again and then went back.

"'If you will be so good as to untie my hands and feet, dear boy, I'll get down and be with you for a glass of good ale or spirits.'

"'Nathan Hale, is that you? Can it be possible? Your voice? Your very self?'

"'Why, of course, my dear friend. Just come and loosen my feet a little—confound those British soldiers—they can't even murder a fellow like gentlemen! They tied me up like a felon!'

"I did as he bid me, and in another moment the old grad. was down by my side off his granite pedestal, kicking off the ropes which bound his feet, and I was untying the cord about his wrists. Gee! he was a well-built chap! and mighty well *bronzed* by wind and weather.

"'Could I get on a foot-ball team?' he asked, with a laugh.

"'Well, I should smile!' I replied.

"'I can do my hundred yards in nine seconds, flat,' he said, stretching out his limbs.

"'Nathan,—Nathan,—don't try to impose upon a credulous mortal!' I laughed, hardly believing my eyes and ears.

"'Can you run with speed?' he asked.

"You chaps know I can do my hundred in eleven seconds—so I thought I'd put the old grad. to the test. I'd heard that he was quite an athlete.

"'I'll race you across City Hall Park,—to the new Court House and back!' I said. 'Come!—for the beer!'

"We started. Well,—I wasn't in it. Fellows, he could have beaten Harry Brooks or any other phenom. we ever could put up. He was a perfect hurricane,—a cyclone. I was badly distanced.

"'Now, as to jumping,' he said, as he came trotting back, 'I've done my twenty-eight feet, often, in camp. I can better that, now,——'

"'Gee Whitaker!' I said. 'Did G. Washington do the measuring? If he did,—why, of course, I'll believe you.'

"'General Washington was my nearest rival,'

he laughed. 'He did his twenty-four feet, I believe, and that was his best.'

"Then just to show what he could do, he just jumped across Broadway, from curb to curb, as light and easy as a bird. I don't know the distance.

"'The beer is on me. Come along, Nat,' said I. 'You're a daisy athlete, and no mistake!' I quite liked the old chap.

" We walked along up Broadway, and he told me that he knew about every Yale man in town now, and gave 'em a friendly glance as they passed. 'I have to keep my stand—and a very high stand too—' he said, ' on my pedestal, all day till twelve. Then I can do what I please till the cocks crow. When they first put me up in City Hall Park, I felt lonely; I thought sure I was in Cork, not York, and all I could see were Irishmen or Italians. But now I know there are *some* Americans here,—and quite a lot of them take off their hats to me, as they pass, and some stop to talk. My office hours, you see, are from sunrise to midnight. I see them on the way to the court house you know, Judge Howland, Tommy Thacher, George Adee, and now and then " Our Chauncey " the "peach"—oh—I know lots of the young Yale graduates too—and they are a'mighty like the fellows in my day—quiet, hard working—with perhaps one case to a dozen young limbs of the law—but a'mighty hopeful.'

"We came to a convenient and handsomely lighted dive and I invited Nat in to have something.

"'The trouble with me is,' said Nat. 'They did n't give me a hat, you see, when I was,—ahem—and, with these bicycle trowsers and long tailed coat, and ruffled shirt—they 'll be apt to fire me out, won't they?'

"'Not on your ambrotype, old man!' I said. 'They 'll take you for a foot-ball player with a chrysanthemum shock. You just say you 're a Yale man,—that 's enough.'

"'Well, it *used* to be so—back in '73,' he said. 'Why—we students used to run old Haven Town in my day——'

"So we went down into a comfortable little place and took seats on either side of a grate fireplace, beside an old mahogany table.

"'What 's your class?' Nat asked me.

"''93.'

"'Just one hundred and twenty years below

me,' he laughed ;—the pleasantest laugh I ever heard. And as he got warm before the fire and the barkeeper made him a glass of hot negus, or some such stuff Nat called it (I throw this in for a historic touch!" laughed Barry—"I took a hot-scotch), his face began to relax, and he smiled as he drank, and said : ' Well, Yale sand seems to be still a drug in the market, from all I hear.'

"'You refer to athletics,—well, yes. We are holding our own pretty well this century, thank you.'

"' It was a pity the war took place just when it did. It spoiled my career as an athlete,' he said. ' I held the mile record in my time. There was an Indian named Uncas,—er —a fellow named Cooper (Yale '06) wrote him up afterwards ; a Delaware,—he did the mile in 3.04—on the shore at Savin Rock. We used to think that pretty good in those days.'

" We had more negus and more hot-scotch. ' If I had time, ' he said, ' I 'd run up and see how the old college has grown. In my day we had just the Chapel and North,—since called South Middle. I roomed my two years in North South, fourth back middle. Jehoshaphat! how

Nat Hale of '73.   163

our boys did catch the war fever! In our class of twenty-three fellows, eleven went to join the Continental Army. The pick of the class went to the war, and how the New Haven belles cried over us! There was a little girl— my stepsister, too——'

" Nat toyed with his negus, musing.

"' There was a little girl with lovely brown eyes,—and she begged and begged me not to go. But I laughed and went. Jehoshaphat! The poor dear little thing cried like her heart would break. That was at New London, you know, where I was at the time teaching school.

"'" You'll never come back, Nat," she said; and I never did, as you know.

"'" Nat Hale," she whispered the last thing in my ear, " Nat Hale,"—she was all pale and trembling, for she fancied she was looking Death in the face ;—" Nat Hale, we shall meet in heaven!"

"'" No, no, Nancy, right here on the shore of New London harbor, where we've often walked beneath the thick maples and pines, and beautiful elms."

"'" Are you prepared, Nat?'"

"'" I hope so . . ." Why, you know, a fellow was n't thinking about dyin' just when he heard a fife an' drum and saw the soldiers marching up the street, off for Boston and Bunker Hill!

"'"Oh, Nat, if I could wear the breeches,—I'd go along with you!" That's just what she said, "Oh, Nat, if I could wear the breeches, I'd go along with you!"

"'Then, I guess I laughed! Ha! ha! I caught the maid in my arms, and such a bussin' and a kissin' she got that day!' Then he sighed, 'Poor soul! Poor soul!

"'For without being promised, sweet Mistress Nancy and I would ha' been wed in secret in due time; nor would I never ha' been a minister neither, as my father wished,—but we planned to be married on the sly and to go down to York,—together,—she and I.

"'Oh, it's the army after all, the army makes the man! and fighting man to man in the field was what I loved, and longed for! Ah me, to get into active service for my country—that was what I longed for.

"'"And," she says, "I fear for you, Nat, and I pray at morning, at noon, and at night for you. And may God be near you in the time of your trial"—she spoke very solemn, I can tell you!

"'"What trial, Nancy? Am I to be tried like a common culprit?—perhaps hanged to a gibbet, ha, ha! for a deserter?"

"'She shuddered, poor girl—"Ah, God,—it's not that;—but in your hour of peril. You are brave and honorable, Nat; you will dare anything for sake of what you call 'glory.' An' I know that a gentleman will go further for glory than common folk, too!" Then you ought, brother Yalensian, t' have seen the tears that dimmed that pair of brown eyes! Tears of pride they were! tears of real old English pride, for we both were English blood to the bone, as you know, and we had the English love of honor,—and we were so soon to be pitted against—Hessians! hirelings!—butchers! Faugh!

"'So I kissed her again, quick, and was off, for I heard down the street and far away the rat-a-tat-tat of the drums.

"'But she hung to me, and clung to me and called me her old pet names and rubbed her smooth little chin against my rough face, and the drums grew louder, and I turned away—

"'Still she held me close to her,—and our love was a secret, mind, for fear of her father by law, and my father too;—and all this was in the forest near City School, at New London, where none could see. A pretty trysting-place,—I fancy it's all gone away now,—long since—long since.

"'And I said,—"Ah, God,"—I said it half roughly, for the drums rang in my ears, and the fever of the war took hold of me. I said, "Come, come, sweet! let me from you! After the war's over and the British driven home to old England,—then there'll be time enough for our billin' and cooin'! Farewell, my little Nancy! Farewell! Farewell!"'

"There was a long silence. I felt really sorry for Nat, for he sighed so deeply.

"'And I never saw her again, but once——'

"He paused and shook with emotion.

"'In the sea of faces behind the row of Hessians—on the field beneath the apple-trees —Rutger's orchard—I looked longingly for a face I knew, an' I heard a cry, "Nat Hale! Nat Hale!" and I saw Her face. Friend, it was sunny with smiles. Friend, she was alone, and then I knew she'd come all the way alone to

New York,—she had run away from home to see the last of me—but the cruel Provost Cunningham would let no one see me,—no, not my own mother!—Oh, how cruel he was! But I *saw* Her. I saw all in a glance, and everything that day was forgotten but love. She had come all the way from New London, where I had been so happy,—and, brave heart, she brought her sweet laughing face to make my last hour less sad. Ah well; they called me a hero,—the people,—I could hear them murmuring like a sullen wind,—but there was a greater hero than I there,—and as I died, I died clasped in spirit in *her* loving arms!

"'What of it! Death is better than dishonor! It was my hard luck, that was all; my luck and some of the old Yale sand, which kept me true to my country. What's Yale is American—that's all; and, there's plenty of the same sand left up there at the old college,—and when wanted,—called for, and ready, too, as I noted in the Civil War——'

"'She married?' I asked.

"Nat frowned. 'She marry? She died of a broken heart, poor child! Do we meet now, you ask ; are we united ? Ah, friend, the after world is but a reflection of life here. I dream and we meet in dreams. She's in the music, in the far mellow ring of bells; she's in the colors of the sunset, in the clouds that float over the river. She lingers in the deep blue of the ocean, —in all that is rare and beautiful—but other than that, she is not. For love such as ours, alas, is only for life, and then it ends.'

"He bowed his head on the table in sorrow.

"In order to be a little more cheerful, I called for more negus and more whisky. Nat said he'd rather like a taste of some old New England rum, as he liked a sip of it when in college very well. The waiter brought a bottle and two glasses.

"'Tell me of your college days——'

"'Oh, like yours, I daresay. Nat Daggett was president. Can we get a pipe do you fancy? Tim Dwight was my tutor.'

"'Here, try one of these cigars; you'll like them.'

"'I've seen Spaniards smoking them, and now I see them on the street,—often. (He lit it and drew in.) Jehoshaphat! That makes me forget my troubles. Dear old Yale! I love thee as much as ever—*in spite* of the Faculty! As old Tim Dwight wrote:

> "'Alma Mater. Here's to thee!
> Nourisher of liberty
> In those parlous times of late,
> When our Nation hung in fate
> Yale! thy sand was useful then,
> Yale! thou borest mighty men.

"'Ah, yes. I was only twenty-one when I died. I graduated when I was eighteen, and we had a great Syllogistic debate. Bill Robinson and I argued for woman's higher education, and won it too! Wish I could hear of Yale's winning an occasional debate with Harvard now-a-days. Ah, we had a splendid class,—old '73. Jim Hillhouse—the finest chap that ever lived; Ez. Samson; Selden of Lyme, a grand chap he; Dave Humphreys;—Wyllys of Hartford; Jack Brown, Sherman, and Huntington,—all those fine fellows. They all went into the war, as I did, and Tallmadge of '73 captured André,— and saw him hanged, as they hanged me. Was n't that odd, now, my friend? Yes, sir, Major Tallmadge and I, we were chums at Yale, and he captured André!

But André was not denied even a Bible on the hour of his death, nor the kind offices of friends, as I was. Ah me, it was a sad, heart-breaking sight to see my last letters of farewell to my mother and sweetheart Nancy burned in my very sight!'

"'You have a glorious name,—deathless,—renowned forever,' I said.

"'I'm very well satisfied *now*. At most, I might have lived to, say 1840, and by this time I would have been fifty years under the sod, in any event. And, too, my name is getting to be better known than ever before. For fifty years my countrymen utterly forgot me. Then came my monument at South Coventry,—and then a statue in Boston, and now one here, where I died, but not on the exact spot. Rutger's orchard was about the corner of East Broadway and Market street. But the old jail, now Hall of Records, still stands where I spent my last night. I was tried and sentenced by Sir William Howe at Fifty-second street and First avenue.

"'And did you die from a cart?'

"'Yes, I was served up *à la carte*,—Ha—ha! I have the laugh on them all now, eh? And

Brute Cunningham, the Provost, to my certain knowledge, is writhing in hell, where he belongs,—All 's well that ends well——'

"' Amen!'

"' And if my death inspired my classmates and fellow soldiers with courage,—it was more useful than my life might have been. The saying, "It 'll all be right in a hundred years!" is true. We realize now that it is moral force and moral strength of character, under God, that is what we are to show on earth. That is what they taught the sons of Eli in my time, and that is what they teach now. Be brave, and true, and honorable, whether called on to die, or live!'

"' Do you know what I 'd like to see? A statue of you on the Yale campus.'

"' Oh, there's no need now. It will come in time, perhaps. I should like it very well. The country has grown rich and great, thousands of foreigners of the poorest class have come in here. It may be well to impress on these the high *value* of free institutions, and with what *difficulty* they were obtained. But I am fully aware that personal liberty is assured for all time and that the new heroes to come will be called on to give up their lives, not for liberty, but for equality and fraternity.'

"Nathan Hale of Yale, '73, rose to go. 'I've enjoyed seeing you, and talking with you, very much,' he said. 'I haven't asked as much as I would like about your recitations, debates, meetings, and your sports. We had a small affair in 1773, like some small school of now-a-days, but we made warm friendships and had our songs and jokes,—and good old rum, too, in spite of the fact that we were, many of us, preparing for the ministry. Oh, yes, we were true college boys,—and boys are the same yesterday, to-day, and forever! Well,—I've got a good many things to do to-night, I've got to walk down to the Treasury building and meet George—for one thing—and I must go.'

"And we shook hands, and with a kindly smile and bow which showed him to be a fine type of the old school gentleman, he was off."

There was a short silence as Barrington finished.

"It's hard to realize that the famous Nathan Hale, the martyr of the Revolution, was after all a hail-fellow-well-met, at college—just like one of us," said Keith.

"Hale of '73. Hail—to thee! He's an honor to the old college! He'd get on the nine and crew and team,—and win the debate with the Harvard for us, too—eh?" cried Little Jack, enthusiastically.

"Yes,—there was nothing Hale of '73 could n't do well," said Barrington, gravely. "Except lying——"

"How's that. That's dead easy!"

"If he'd been clever at that, the British never would have captured him. But he had a sort of high and mighty disdain for deceit,—and, like a gentleman, he owned up at once what he was,—a spy."

"He *was* a gentleman!" said Keith.

Little Jack shook his head. "He was n't in the right place then, and George Washington underestimated his man when he let him act as a spy. He belonged way up,—he ought to have been made a general. Why, they threw away too valuable a man, fellows; I say it was a shame!"

Little Jack Horner began to get excited.

"I say it was a shame and a sin to let that noble-hearted old grad. of '73 go and play spy as he did. Why in the name of all the prophets did n't they send a nigger? Any one would have done better than he. Yes, sir, he was too great a man!"

"Why then,—to act as he did then, he was far and away the grandest old grad. Yale has ever had!"

"Well,—he just was ;—he was square, modest, gentle, good-hearted, brave, plucky with the 'sand' of a lot of pure-minded Puritan ancestors. Gad! He was the greatest Yale man that ever lived!" said Barrington simply.

And, after a little, the talk fell on other matters.

THE DAWN TEA.

Scene :—A cozy student's room in Lawrance Hall. Time 4.30 A.M. of the morning after the Prom.
Present, in evening dress, Mrs. Montgomery, Chaperon ; Miss Helen Montgomery, Miss Clara Powers, Miss Kitty Nelson, some of the usual crowd of Seniors. The girls look more or less worn and fagged, and have just come from the Prom.
(A side table, on which cups and saucers are set out and tea is steeping, and several bottles of iced champagne are standing wrapped in napkins, and glasses, presided over by Honest John, the college sweep, in an alpaca coat and clean white apron.)

Mrs. Montgomery [*doing her duty as chaperon, throwing off her heavy opera cloak*]. Are you quite sure, Mr. Paige, that the sun rises, as you say, at five? This making a night of it is a little wearisome. I feel quite dragged. [*Sinks into a chair and pulls off her gloves.*]

Little Jack Horner [*aside*]. Poor old dragon! [*Goes about turning up several pretty lamps, half concealed in deep red, white, and yellow shades.*]

Miss Montgomery [*turning to Miss Powers,*

whispers anxiously]. Clara, I'm dead with sleep;—do tell me how I look?

Miss Powers. Like a funeral, dear;—and I?

Miss Montgomery. Like a last week's "American Beauty." [*Both smile sweetly.*]

Boots Paige [*concealing a yawn*]. Poor Mrs. Montgomery! [*Turning to her.*] Have you enjoyed the Prom.?

Mrs. Montgomery. Very much. I have a way of sleeping, you know. I can fall asleep anywhere,—sometimes it is positively ludicrous! Thanks, no champagne for me. [*Honest John passes around a tray on which are half a dozen glasses.*]

[*Under the Red Lamp.*]

Miss Kitty Nelson [*politely conceals a yawn*]. It was a jolly ball,—not quite so eventful as last year's. [*Takes a glass of champagne.*]

Sprague. No. I should say not! [*Aside to her.*] I wish you wouldn't, Kitty. You know what I think about it.

Miss Kitty [*smiles, and puts aside the glass untasted*]. But I enjoyed it better. [*Turning to the chaperon.*] When one's engaged, Mrs. Montgomery, one dances with a positive fury,

The Dawn Tea.

—knowing that the opportunities are growing less.

[*Mrs. Montgomery* [*drowsily*]. But, my dear, —there are—married—balls. [*She closes her eyes as if exhausted.*]

Miss Kitty. Unfortunately not for us!

Mrs. Montgomery. Three days of this sort of thing,—I fear will be the death of me.

Little Jack Horner. Poor dear lady!—The dawn tea appears to be just the feather that breaks the dragon's back!

Miss Kitty. We expect to live in Ohio, don't we, Dick, dear? and out there I fancy marriages and deaths are the same thing.

Little Jack [*teasingly*]. Poor girl! Why do you marry the Dwarf, anyway? He deprives you of the fizz, and it's ten to one he does n't really love you a little bit——

Miss Kitty. Perhaps. It was only half-past nine when he last vowed and declared he did.

Sprague. Don't listen to him, Kitty!

Miss Helen Montgomery [*from the corner of the sofa*]. Do nudge mamma, some one, and keep her awake. It is *awful*. This is in the midst of college, and we are surrounded by hundreds,—thousands of men——

Miss Powers. Surrounded,—but we'll never surrender!

[*They nudge Mrs. Montgomery, gently.*]

Mrs. Montgomery [*opening her eyes, and trying to look very wide awake*]. These dawn teas, as you call them, are quite new, they say. They are very nice, jolly affairs,—very—jolly! Just at this time if one cannot sleep—a little nourishment is quite necessary. Have you any bouillon?—I never drink champagne.

[*A tray is passed around by Honest John the Thief, containing bouillon, Russian tea, candies, fruits, preserves, biscuits, cake, etc.*]

Mrs. Montgomery. Really, what a variety— Do you get all these things from commons?

Little Jack. No,—only the spoons.

[*Under the Yellow Lamp.*]

Miss Clara Powers. Yes, there are lots of things—such bright things,—one remembers just *after* one has left the floor,—and now one has a chance to get them off,—I believe that's the *raison d'être* of a dawn tea.

Little Jack Horner. Then be good natured and say some of those bright things,—it may keep us awake!

LAWRANCE HALL.

Miss Clara. Really,—I have n't thought them up yet,—I am not feeling particularly clever, just now—That is—Dear me! I danced every dance!

"*Austin* [*sentimentally*]. Like a beautiful fairy! Ah, Miss Powers, my heart, etc,. etc. If you only *knew*, etc., etc.

Miss Clara [*sedately*]. Don't!—Really,—I am over tired as it is, Mr. Austin.

Little Jack [*as Austin tremblingly pours out a glass of champagne*]. Why do you tremble so, Adolphus?

Austin. My best girl has just shook me! [*Laughter.*]

Miss Clara. You refer to me? How I wish I *could!*

Tad Nelson [*handing around a tray of tea and Educators—whispers*]. For Heaven's sake, Jack, drink some tea and stimulate your brain. We depend on you to keep things going, you know, and things are going slow as molasses——

Little Jack [*making a brace*]. I heard quite a poor thing gotten off by Aldrich, of our class. He's a great chess man, you know,—he said he'd given up two knights to one queen. [*Yawns.*] I thought he'd made a poor exchange.

Miss Clara. Who is Mr. Aldrich's "queen," at present?

Little Jack [*thoughtfully*]. Well,—I know who *was!* I think he's with her somewhere now, wandering about on his way here. [*Yawns.*] I say, [*with an effort to be entertaining*] on the whole, dawn tea cups are not what they are cracked up to be. [*A sympathetic silence.*]

[*Little Jack looks hopelessly around the room. Barrington and Miss Montgomery are seated on the window seat. Miss Montgomery's eyes are closed.*]

Little Jack. I say, Great, you're not in a prize fight! Trying to put your opponent to sleep?

Barrington. No, but see, I have closed both her eyes!

Miss Montgomery [*awaking suddenly*]. Er—what?—Oh, as you were saying, er—

Paige [*in a loud cheerful voice*]. Have some sandwiches,—some of the pâté, Miss Montgomery. By the way, your mother is peacefully asleep again, and we've gently, but firmly led her into an adjoining room, to sleep undisturbed;—we chatter too much in here. It is no time to chatter, but to eat, sleep, and try to be merry.

Miss Montgomery. And we are unchaperoned! O heavens! [*Rises as if to go to her mother.*]

Paige [*with assumed earnestness*]. Let *me* be your chaperon—confide in me—What is it?

Miss Montgomery [*putting her hand up to her hair*]. I think I've danced my hair down, for one thing.

Paige. Well, I'll be switched!

Miss Montgomery [*laughing*] You are *so* funny, Mr. Paige!

Tad Nelson [*goes to window*]. But see! the rosy fingers of dawn are upon the morning sky! It's getting brighter! [*Yawns.*]

Little Jack. Yes,—I wish *we* were! [*Turning to several girls.*] Won't you have some champagne?

Chorus of girls. No,—we've decided not to—It's bad form——

Little Jack. To drink anything but cocktails at this hour—But how did *you* know?

Chorus of girls. You are perfectly horrid!

[*The door opens and in walks Miss Eleanor*

Swift, shivering with the cold, with Laze Aldrich, the latter in a heavy fur-lined ulster.]

Chorus. Well,—where have you been?

Miss Swift. Foraging. [*Looks about.*] Where is,—is—Mrs. Montgomery—Oh, I'm nearly dead.

Chorus. The chaperon is asleep—Hush!

Miss Swift [*shivering*]. We got lost, did n't we, Mr. Aldrich, and we'd no idea where you all were. [*Throws off her wrap.*] Oh, I'm as hungry and tired as a Feejee missionary. I am danced out,—spun out,—talked out,—laughed out,——

Little Jack. Put out?

Miss Swift. Not yet—Expect to be if I hang on here at Yale much longer!

Little Jack [*laughing*]. Oh, no, you will never be fired,—you're not wicked enough for that!

Aldrich. You see,—we thought you were all over at Battersby's tea in Durfee, and we went there. They yawned graveyards at us,—and made us tired. And so we went to Jim Allen's tea in Farnam. All asleep in chairs there,—plates in their laps,—woke them up! It looked like a field of battle after the fight—

the dead and wounded waiting to be carried away. Oh, these dawn teas are the stuff!

[*Under the White Lamp.*]

Miss Swift [*seating herself in an easy chair*]. Tell me who invented the dawn tea? It is so very weird!

Little Jack. It is certainly not what you'd call a rum idea,—is it!

Miss Swift. That depends! [*Hastily.*] I think the man who invented the dawn tea should be hoist in his own teapot!

Paige. Yes; hung, quartered,—and *drawn.*

Aldrich. I think it came in with the beautiful and pathetic song, *You can't leave me, Charlie!* [*Laughter.*]

Miss Swift. Never saw such devotion the last two days in all my life. As I said to Mr. Aldrich,—" are we *never* to part?"

Aldrich. And I said, you remember, "No," and then you said, "Ah, me,—it's just like heaven, then, isn't it?"

Miss Swift [*indignantly*]. Mr. Aldrich, you have a brilliant imagination!

Aldrich [*half whispers*]. To *me* it would be heaven!

Paige [*opening the heavy curtains and letting in the gray morning light*]. Poor girls! Poor girls! Prithee, why so pale? Wait! Let me turn the colloseum on to Juliet!

Aldrich [*whispers to Paige*]. Something must be done! It's awful slow—What shall we do to wake them up?

Paige. Play our last trump!

[*Aldrich winks and hovers for a moment over the red tea cups arranged on the tray. Honest John the Thief laughs, and Aldrich thumps him on the back.*]

Honest John. Dat's de greatest impositium dat I eber see played;—dat red tea is queered! Hi! hi!

Aldrich [*whispers*]. Shut up, you black rascal! Keep dark! Be sure and serve the red cups only to the men,—do you hear? I wouldn't have the ladies drink it, of course,—for anything in the world. Remember, the cognac is in the *red* cups only.

Miss Montgomery [*leans back in her chair*]. I wonder where papa is. You know, he always calls for us and takes us home. It's a way he has. And what will he say to poor mamma's deserting the ship?

Little Jack. That the dawn tea was too great a hardship.

Miss Montgomery [*seriously*]. Papa is a clergyman, you know.

Paige [*aside to Miss Swift*]. Really! that's nothing against him! At least he can give us a benediction!

Honest John the Thief [*passing around the tray of Russian tea*]. De blue cups is ladies', ma'm, yes, ma'm——

Miss Montgomery [*sipping, but not drinking*]. It seems rather weak. It needs more steeping, Mr. Aldrich, and more lemon, and more——

Aldrich [*laughing to himself*]. Oh, does it? Well, the next will be—stronger.

Miss Powers. *I* think it's too strong. [*Barely tastes the tea.*]

Miss Swift [*who has quietly insisted upon taking a red cup*]. It's delicious, Mr. Aldrich,—but it isn't tea—it's punch. [*Tries to look indignant.*]

Aldrich. It's gin-seng. Don't say a word!

[*Under the Red Lamp.*]

Miss Kitty Nelson [*returning from an obscure corner with Sprague*]. Oh, give me a red cup.

One lump, please. [*Drinks.*] How refreshing Russian tea is! [*Looks at Paige.*] You wicked boy!

Paige. Hush! 'T was n't me,—as done it! It's only for us fellows, anyway! Don't give the tea away!

Kitty. No, I want it myself. But you can tell it by its breath.

Paige. Yes,—*we* can!—*we old,*—ahem! *They* can't, the innocents!

Kitty [*provoked*]. I'm going to warn everybody the red tea is drugged!

Paige. No, don't! Perhaps they know it, and like it; and if you do,—they won't want to take any more,—and you'll get yourself disliked!

Kitty [*laughs*]. Very true; it's good, anyway.

Little Jack. And thus you've begun to pull the wool over the eyes of the poor Dwarf!

Kitty. Hush!

Aldrich [*beckoning Little Jack aside and indicating Miss Powers and Austin*]. Listen to them! They are getting gay! And Adolphus is just *as* innocent, too! What are we going to do?

[*They approach Austin who is seated on the sofa next Miss Powers and who, by way of a joke, has innocently exchanged cups with her.*]

Miss Powers [*drinks from the red cup*]. Oh, that last waltz—tum-tum—da-da [*gestures with her cup*]. I wish we could dance now—ah me! Waldteufel's divine waltzes!

Austin. Only divine while they embodied you! [*Swallows his tea giddily.*]

Miss Powers [*swinging dance card in her hand*]. I could dance it all over again—*da capo.*

Austin. You have danced your way into my heart. [*Sighs.*]

Miss Powers. Then I'm sure it's high time I've danced out again—for I feel quite stifled!

Austin. To be sure I'm not an omnibus!

Miss Powers. No! [*Laughing.*] You must be taken in small courses, *à la cart!*

Little Jack [*to Aldrich*]. Yes,—capital horse on Adolphus, isn't it?

Aldrich [*anxiously*]. But Miss Powers must never know it!

Paige [*as he swallows his tea*]. I feel like saying what the freshman who once took dinner with Prexy said——

Miss Montgomery. What's that?

Paige. Let's have another! [*Helps himself from the tray.*]

[*A knock. Enter Rev. Dr. Montgomery, naturally very cold, glum, and sour.*]

Rev. Dr. Montgomery. Nellie! Are you aware of the hour? What! Champagne? [*Scowls.*] I hardly approve of this.

[*Honest John is told to hide away the bottles.*]

Miss Montgomery [*gayly*]. Poor papa! You ought to be home and in bed!

Rev. Dr. Montgomery. Is this fitting? Is this seemly? Where is your mother?

Miss Montgomery. She's asleep!

[*Austin, Aldrich, Barrington, etc., grasp his hand with greatest unction and help him off with his overcoat, for Miss Nellie is a very pretty girl.*]

Rev. Dr. Montgomery. I have the carriage waiting——

Barrington [*politely trying to entertain the old gentleman*]. You are an old grad., sir, are you not? Of the famous class of Umpty which?

Rev. Dr. Montgomery [*a little mollified*]. Yes. Umpty-one,—the greatest class that ever graduated at Yale. But, come, Nellie. Come, at once!

Paige. But you'll have a glass of champagne, Doctor?

Rev. Dr. Montgomery [*puts out his hand in rebuke*]. Certainly not! Certainly not!

Barrington. Won't you have some tea?

Rev. Dr. Montgomery No,—we can't wait, and I don't like tea.

Miss Swift. I'm sure mine was awfully strong. [*Rises.*] But I feel quite,—oh, much better. Really—quite giddy.

Miss Clara Powers [*rising to go*]. I don't feel a bit tired now——

Austin. Dear Miss Clara—I—must mention to you before we part,—gi—oh, gi me back me heart! etc., etc.

Miss Clara [*vexedly*]. Oh, take it! and *do* hold on to it,—in future. Really, Mr. Austin!

Rev. Dr. Montgomery [*solemnly*]. The carriage is waiting. Really it is very late. Come, Nellie——

Paige [*cordially*]. Have just one cup of Russian tea, Doctor? [*Hands red cup and saucer.*]'

Rev. Dr. Montgomery [*sternly*]. I don't care for tea.

Paige. But Really. Won't you try just one cup?

Rev. Dr. Montgomery. Well,—I will take just one [*Sips his tea slowly.*] Where *is* your mother, Nellie? I have had a distressing time finding you. These gayeties were n't known in *my* day. And they are apparently like Heber's Sabbath—without end.

Miss Montgomery. Mamma!! [*No response.*] Mamma!!!

[*She opens the door, looks in, and then looks back into the room with a face of blank despair. The doctor drinks his tea at a swallow.*]

Rev. Dr. Montgomery. I never cared—er—for Russian tea. But that is quite good—very refreshing——

Aldrich. Have another, Doctor?

Rev. Dr. Montgomery. I don't mind,—the cups are not large. Please, not quite so much sugar,—only one lump, please. And really, I prefer milk, if you have it.

Aldrich. Oh, very good. [*Prepares another stiff cup, with some milk, which the doctor innocently swallows.*]

Rev. Dr. Montgomery. Well now, my dear. Call your mother and let's be off. Ahem!

very good tea that—excellent—Very refreshing—very invigorating——

Little Jack [*mischievously*]. Before we go,—we ought to have a song.

Rev. Dr. Montgomery. That tea was very warming—very—[*Toys with his spoon.*]

Little Jack [*aside*]. He likes it!

Aldrich. Give us an old-time Yale song, Doctor,—one of your time——

Rev. Dr. Montgomery. Oh, dear me;—I've forgotten all the songs I ever knew in the '50s. Let me see—[*Hums a few notes.*]

Little Jack [*aside*]. This is rich!

Miss Montgomery [*anxiously to Jack*]. Was it really *tea* papa drank?

Little Jack. What does it matter?

Miss Montgomery. I shall be very indignant if——

Little Jack. I assure you, solemnly, it was rushing good tea!

[*Rev. Dr. Montgomery after a little urging sings Dr. Holmes' old song in a loud basso, to the tune of "Off the Blue Canaries."*]

"And who was on the Catalogue
When College was begun?

> Two nephews of the President
>   And the Professor's son.
> (They turned a little Indian down
>   As brown as any bun. . . .)
> Lord! how the Seniors knocked about
>   That freshman class of one!"

[Loud applause—Mrs. Montgomery wakes up and comes to the door and stands astonished.]

> "They had not then the dainty things
>   That Prom. weeks now afford,
> But succotash and hominy
>   Were smoking on the board.
> They did not rattle round in cabs,
>   Or dash in long-tailed blues—
> But always on Commencement days—
>   The tutors blacked their shoes!"

[Loud applause again.]

Miss Swift [*behind her handkerchief*]. How very weird!

Mrs. Montgomery. Why, William! *You* singing! I never heard you sing before.

Rev. Dr. Montgomery. Oh, when I'm at Yale, Eliza, I only feel as old as when I was a student. Hark! There strikes the Chapel bell. I remember the appropriate lines of my classmate Bradley:

The Dawn Tea.

[*Recites feelingly amid deep silence when the first bell rings.*]

" 'T is the hour for deep contrition,
 'T is the hour for peaceful thought,
 'T is the hour to win the blessing
 In the early stillness sought.
 Kneeling in the quiet chamber,
 On the deck, or on the sod,—
 In the still and early morning—
 'T is the hour to worship God.

" But don't stop to pray in secret,—
 No time for *you* to worship here,—
 The hour approaches,—*tempus fugit*,—
 Tear your shirt,—or miss a prayer,—
 Don't stop to wash,—don't stop to button,—
 Go the ways your father's trod,
 Leg it,—put it,—rush it,—streak it,—
 Run and worship God!

" On the staircase stamping, tramping,
 Bounding, sounding, crashing smashing,
 Jumping, bumping, dancing, dashing,
 Jarring, stubbing heel and toe—
 See your classmates chase before you
 Through the Chapel doorway jam—
 Heavens and Earth!—the bell is stopping!
 Now it dies in silence———damn! !"

[*Loud applause from the men.*]

Chorus of girls. Oh, how shocking!—that last line!

Paige. Here's to the class of Umpty-one!

Rev. Dr. Montgomery. Yes; it numbers Jones, the famous poet, and Smith, the great astronomer.

Barrington [*laughing aside*]. Never heard of either of them, did you, Jack?

Rev. Dr. Montgomery. Then there was our brave Col. Jack Petterson, who gave up his life for his country. Did you ever hear the story? He was suddenly surrounded at the picket line by the enemy, one night. It was in Georgia. They were making a secret night attack on the left wing of Sherman's army. A rebel officer held a sword at his breast. "If you make any noise, you're a dead man!" he whispered. "I'll run you through the body!" Col. Jack Petterson knew if he did not give the alarm of the approaching enemy, Sherman's army might be cut in pieces. It was a question of certain death or the betrayal of ten thousand men. He stepped back and shouted: "*The rebels are on us!*" And then fell dead, pierced through the heart. But the alarm was given.

The army was saved. That was one of many things Yale did in the war for the Union!

[*A short silence.*]

Little Jack. That's a dandy! Oh, I wonder if it's true. Here's to Col. Jack Petterson!

Barrington. Let me fill your cup once more, Doctor! [*Pours out another cup full.*]

Little Jack [*chuckling*]. Fill mine, too!

Rev. Dr. Montgomery. No, we must be going. [*Drinks his tea quickly.*] I never seemed to care for tea before in my life. Come, my dear, come, Nellie! Come, all! Say good morning!

Mrs. Montgomery [*greatly refreshed by her nap*]. I hope my duties are now over for the week?

Little Jack. Were they very arduous?

Mrs. Montgomery. I once took a walking tour with my husband in Switzerland. . . .

Chorus of girls. Good night—Great fun—Awful good time! Don't feel sleepy a bit. Splendid tea!

Miss Kitty Nelson. Never enjoyed myself so much in my life! But I shall be very glad—er—to get Dick away from you all. I don't trust you. You students are very wicked!

Little Jack. Wicked!!

Miss Kitty. But I must say—a dawn tea without,—ahem,—*something wicked*, never will be a success in the world! Good morning!

Rev. Dr. Montgomery. I feel like going home and writing a sermon on the influence of tea upon the moral instincts! Good morning!

[*Exeunt the doctor, his wife, and the girls, amid great laughter, while the Chapel bell rings and the students jump into their ulsters and are off to Battell on the run.*]

THE GREAT SPRINGFIELD GAME.

THE old grads. who live in and around New York, and haunt the University Club, and who get the athletic fever in their old bones once a year, and who always have lots of advice on tap but who do pretty well (as well as age will permit) in supporting the Yale teams on their annual appearance, have this story to tell of the great game at Springfield a year ago.

Every one remembers what an exciting game it was, and how hard fought it was, and how the event hung in the balance through the two halves and was only decided in Yale's favor by a goal won at the close of the game. And every one remembers, too, how terrific the battle was, and how clearly it demonstrated that full-grown men cannot play the so-called Rugby game without real danger to life and limb.

A number of these old Yale grads. had arranged, several weeks before, to charter a drawing-room car, and to stock it well with fizz and a capital lunch, and they looked forward to the game with great anticipations. Most of them, as was their wont, had managed to get bets out of Harvard grads. of fifty dollars or so—enough to pay expenses in case of success.

The morning of the great Saturday came, and the sun rose bright, and the weather was perfect. The grads. sank into their comfortable pivot chairs as the train left the Grand Central Depot, and swung into the tunnel with the most agreeable expectations.

There were several old foot-ball players in the car. Old "Popper" Hardy, "Steve" Anderson, and "Billy" Simmons. They were the ex-heroes of hard-fought games in their day and generation, and had sunk into the innocuous desuetude of private life, after their four years of public recognition and celebrity, not without some real regret. But the great game brought most of them out of their holes, and at Springfield you could generally tell the old players by their extra official excitement and their intense, feverish interest in every play made. They were "in the game" from start to finish. There were other ex-backers of the team, too; busy lawyers, doctors, business men, now, who

The Great Springfield Game.   199

once went up with the gang from New Haven, and shouted themselves hoarse with the Aristophanian cry of their day. Life had been gentle and easy with most of them,—they were "doing fairly well," and generally had a little spare cash to put on the Yale team every year.

Among these were Dr. Trunnion, Pete Jones, a Virginian, Sam Callendar, Charley Macy, Harry Whalley, and some other good fellows.

They talked together of old times and the glorious record of Yale, and what an extraordinary thing it was that time and age did not seem to wither nor custom stale their old enthusiasm, and how they enjoyed the foot-ball games now even more than ever before, although they understood them less.

"Why," said Dr. Trunnion, a fat-faced, jolly old grad. of the class of Umpty-one, "I really think I could n't miss a Springfield game now for love or money. It 's got to be an annual thing with me. I tell my wife that unless I 'm present our boys would n't win. I 'm a sort of mascot, you see."

"I sometimes willingly let all the ball games and the race go," said Sam Callendar, "but I can't miss the Harvard game at Springfield. It's the most exciting of all, by all odds."

"Yes,—and it's the first big game of the year," said Whalley, "and you see the new tricks brought out,—and the field is the best in America,—and,—the day is always clear, and,—I would n't miss it for ducats."

"Oh, no," chimed in Pete Jones, a splendid specimen of Virginia manhood. "I myself ought to have gone on to Washington to-day, —may lose a thousand dollars by coming up, —but I would n't miss seeing Harvard downed again for all the law business in the country."

Thereupon, *pour passer le temps*, as Macy suggested, they opened a bottle.

Popper Hardy joined them, and roused the enthusiasm for their *Alma Mater* to almost a fighting pitch by describing one of the old-time hard-fought foot-ball games down at the old polo grounds on One Hundred and Tenth street, in New York.

"There 's one thing," said Dr. Trunnion, with a sagacious shake of his wise old head, "they would n't do so well if it were not for us old grads. We follow up the games, and keep them at it year to year."

The Great Springfield Game. 201

Then they drank toasts to the old grads. and to Yale, and to the success of the blue.

As the train swung along past Stamford a "little game" was suggested to fill up the time, and they went into the smoking compartment, and the good-natured colored porter set up a table.

They used matches for chips, and presently the little game began to grow interesting. Every one was smoking; every one had his hat on the back of his head; every one was silent. Dr. Trunnion was doing the winning and seemed to have a comfortable monopoly of the luck.

"Poker is a great game, if played scientifically," he frequently remarked.

At New Haven there was a great deal of demonstration going on at the station and a crowd of noisy students were rah, rah-ing to considerable extent. There was nearly thirty dollars in the jack-pot, and Callendar had opened it with a pair of queens.

"For Heaven's sake, what is all this fuss about here at New Haven?" asked Macy. "Close that window, won't you, Doctor?"

The window was promptly closed and the game went on.

They reached Springfield in due time and, of course, every one else in the car got out. The poker players, however, were hitting the game up at that time and had put down nearly a bottle of fizz apiece.

The doctor had started in to lose the pile he had accumulated when the train was at New Haven, and Macy was winning now in a canter. Callendar was borrowing chips. Pete Jones was doing a moderate amount of bluffing and holding his pile "stiddy." Whalley was very silent, but was slightly ahead of the game. The "special" train was side-tracked in the railroad freight yard at Springfield, ready to be started back after the foot-ball game was over.

All the five grads. were old poker players but the matches bothered them a good deal in counting, and so the porter was given five dollars out of the pot, and sent out to scour the city of Springfield for a stack of ivories.

He came back after awhile, with a broad grin on his comely black face.

" "Youse gents won't see no foot-ball game, ef you don't hurry along," he said. "It's pretty much after two."

But they told him they'd only play one

hand around and get to Hampden Park before the players got fairly warmed up.

The new chips enlivened the game, and the doctor secretly hoped, would change the luck also.

They played another hand, and the doctor won and felt greatly comforted.

Then they decided they 'd have a jack-pot, and get out. It was half-past two.

The jack-pot went on accumulating, as jack-pots have a little way of doing, and it took some time before Whalley opened it with a pair of aces.

They all came in. Whalley drew three, the doctor drew three. Pete stood pat and Callendar and Macy two each, and the betting and and bluffing began. All seemed to feel very earnestly, too, that they had extraordinarily goods hands. "Raise it five," or "Raise it ten," were the only expressions used for some time. Finally Pete counted out all the chips he had on the table,—about fifty-five dollars' worth,— and it came to be a question of staying in or going out and losing what each had put in. Whalley went down in his pockets and "coughed up," as he said, enough to call.

The doctor came in and saw them. Macy went out in disgust, and on showing up, it was found that Pete held three nines and scooped the pot.

They could n't let Pete win all the cash around the table and they concluded to have one more jack and quit.

After considerable delay,—the cards were not running high,—Pete dealt a pair of aces to Macy and he opened at twenty-five. Every one came in and drew cards and the pot went to the doctor on a full hand, jacks and threes. He netted nearly two hundred dollars.

It was then nearly three, and Macy said as it was hardly worth while to try and see the end of the first half, they 'd have plenty of time for another jack-pot. So they played another, as men will do, fascinated by the enticing game, and then another and another until it began to grow dark.

The luck had varied a good deal and Macy was now ahead and only Whalley was "out" to any very great extent. As Whalley was in excellent circumstances and had recently made a heavy fee in a corporation case, he was in no hurry to stop, feeling the old gambler's fever

The Great Springfield Game. 205

to get even in the way he 'd got " out." The game went on steadily and presently they began to hear excited voices outside the car. Then some one burst in on them and shouted:

" By Jove! I 'll be d——d! You 're a nice set of Yale men, *you* are!"

Keep quiet, won't you?" said the doctor, angrily.

" Don't you care to hear who 's won?" asked the new-comer.

" I 'll open it with a pair of jacks," said Callendar, with the monotonous voice of the steady player.

" You 'd sit here,—you five,—and see your old college beaten twenty to nothing!—" groaned the new-comer, a more recent grad. than they. "You 're a nice set, you are!" and he left disgusted.

" Beaten?" said Pete. "Glad we were n't there!" and they all laughed.

" Raise you ten," said Whalley.

" See it,—and raise five," said Pete.

And so the game went on.

Then more got on the car, shouting, singing, and happy with victory.

" Gad!—you fellows have got back to your

game here mighty quick!" said one, as he lit a cigar. "Wasn't it grand to have made that last goal!"

"Ante up, Pete!" called Whalley, who had begun to win again.

"Yale, Yale! Rah! Rah! Rah!"

And then the crowd surged in and broke up the game. Men were laughing and crying. Men and girls waving blue flags got in the wrong car,—it didn't matter,—Yale had won! Every one wanted some fizz at once, to drink to Yale, Yale, Yale—forever! And the train started, and there was nothing but noise and enthusiasm henceforth all the way to New York.

Pete, turning to Callendar, said, laughing, "Say, Cal, this yere foot-ball fever is a d——d nuisance, is n't it?" [*He was in a cool thousand.*]

"No," said Callendar, ruefully [*he was out about one hundred and ninety dollars*]. "I think we have been a set of d——d fools, Pete."

Whalley, the "Dock," and Macy each swore it was the last game of poker they 'd play for a week of Sundays.

Up at one end of the car, Judge Holler of '52, was up on a chair for a speech, and there was silence.

"All credit to our brave eleven who won us the game," he cried. "But remember that we old grads. had something to do with it. It was *our* enthusiasm, *our* money, *our* backing that helped to win that terrible game. It was because we men of New York put aside our business, and came up here to Springfield to cheer on our boys, ["*Hear! Hear!*" shouted *Pete Jones*]——that helped to win!" and so forth, and so forth, and there was more rah, rah-ing and more popping of corks. No one shouted louder or applauded harder than the poker fiends. In the excitement of victory they escaped the penalty of their misdeeds.

And so the poker enthusiasts each agreed to keep the great Springfield game very quiet, and they hoped nothing would be said about it. But somehow it has all leaked out, and they say they gave a dinner to the eleven after the Princeton game, at the club, by way of satisfying their reproving consciences.

IN THE TOILS OF THE ENEMY.

"LITTLE JACK" HORNER had been on to Cambridge over Sunday, visiting his old Andover chum, and a number of his friends gathered in his room in Lawrance the night he arrived, to hear the latest news of the Harvard nine and crew.

There was a Freshman present, a brother of Little Jack's chum, Keith, and the little chap enlarged some of his story probably, to fit young Keith's youthful imagination.

"You know they've changed the Latin motto on their University seal now to an English one," he said gravely. "It used to be '*Christo et Ecclesiæ Veritas*,'—a very pretty motto. It is now in English, 'To h—l with Yale!'"

The Freshman grinned, but was silent.

"And I found out how they have been winning the annual debate right along, too."

"How is that?"

"They have rung in professionals on us."

"Oh,—come off!"

"Fact, 'I assure you,' as they say on the stage. They have raised a fund of ten thousand dollars and have hunted up professional debaters; two of them are distinguished ex-prize fighters,—and they are taking a course in the Harvard Dental School. Oh, it's all wrong,—and should be stopped. But of course, 'anything to beat Yale.' They have men out all through the West hunting up new debaters,—and they say up there now, that their best men don't care to go in for athletics,—and that chess and debating are intellectual pursuits, and that Yale is way behind the times. Gad! I don't know but they are right. But we've got to win a debate soon, or something will happen——The talkers are all tending to Harvard now as it is. They can out-talk us two to one!"

"How about the crew?"

"Oh, the crew—well, the word was passed around, I suppose, that I was on to get a line on them, and so they put up a job. As an ex-cox. of a winning Yale eight, they treated me very white, and took me all over the boat-house, and showed me everything. They are a smooth set of men, this year's crew, and know their business. It was their hour of practice, so they got into their boat and rowed up the river, then turned and went down, very fast."

" Well, how was it?"

Little Jack began to laugh. "I never saw anything quite like it. Every man rowed a stroke of his own. Every one was pulling out of the boat, and the crew was made up of the queerest assorted sizes you ever saw. Right in the waist they had a man not much over five feet high, and next to him was a seven-footer, (number five). Bow was too fat for a boat, in my judgment; he must have weighed two hundred and fifty pounds. Every one was serious about it,—but if that was the H. U. 'Varsity crew, why——"

"It was a fake crew, Jack."

"Perhaps it was,—but it was all I could do to keep from laughing. They politely asked me to criticize the crew. But it was so d——d bad I couldn't. Then they got me to put on a sweater and got me out to cox a scrub crew, —and they splashed me so much, I feel wet yet! Then we all went over to the Porc. Club and had unlimited fizz, and I sang a song by request, and they got me to telling yarns, and one of the chappies called on me for my Great American Pie Story and I gave 'em that and told them how I was run over by a funeral in Philadelphia, and then, midst loud and continued applause, I gave them this. It happened in New London last year and I never told it to a soul before, but as it was a good horse on me, I told it then to the Harvards—and you fellows shall have it too.

"You see I knew some of those dear Harvard boys almost as well as I know you and Bob. Fales and Jack Rattleton and Dick Eaton and Holworthy and Stoughton were all Andover men, and when I took my aunt and sister to the Pequot, I found the gang all there, but without a cent for betting purposes, in the usual Harvard style. Some had sailed down in yachts, some had cat-boats, and the night *before* the race, they celebrated a good deal, in the usual Harvard way.

"They helped smash in the bar and then undertook to play horse with me and tossed me around a bit, on the lawn in front of the Pequot, and they got me to sing, and we all sang, and we all went to bed pretty well sprung that night, to my deep regret.

"The hotel was crowded, and my aunt and sister had a room just opposite to mine on the top floor. Some of the Harvard men had a room next to mine and I foolishly unbolted the door between. Well, there was more horse play and foolishness up to about three o'clock A.M. and then things quieted down, and when I woke up it was broad daylight and I was utterly alone.

"The race was to be at eleven o'clock. I jumped out of bed and looked at my watch on the bureau,—it was nearly ten! I felt rather seedy and stumbled about looking for my clothes,—Gad! my valise and everything was gone! I rang the bell, but in the excitement downstairs, I suppose, no one answered it. I looked in the next room. I looked out in the hall,—there was n't a soul in sight. My aunt and sister were not in their room. (I supposed they would give me an awful lecture when I saw them.) I opened the window and looked out. Crowds of people were walking toward the wharf to take the boat to the race.

"What was I to do? Those Harvard friends of mine thought it a good joke on me, I suppose, to steal my clothes and take themselves off to the race without waking me up. I tried to call a chambermaid, but there was n't one in sight,—and I don't know what I should have done in my anguish, when, thank the Lord, I heard a tap at my door, and went to it——

"'Will, do hurry!' It was my sister's voice. 'Aunt won't go to the race,—please hurry! We 'll have to go without her.'

"'They 've stolen all my clothes, Molly,— those Harvard fellows——'

"'Have n't you anything——?' she asked through the keyhole.

"'Not a thing, dear. I 'm posing in the "altogether"!'

"'Oh, Will! it 's a just punishment to you after last night!—The noise was dreadful!'

"'Perhaps it is,' I said, 'But don't preach now, sister dear—get me something to put on. I want to see the race——'

"'I have n't anything,—except some dresses, —and one of Aunt's.'

"'Get me Aunt Sarah's black silk,' I cried, 'I have n't seen "Charlie's Aunt" for nothing! I 'll wear anything rather than not see the race! and it 's half past ten nearly now.'

"Well, Molly had seen 'Charlie's Aunt' too,

and she laughed and caught on to the idea in great shape. She flung me my aunt's dress and a lace cap and bonnet. I put 'em on over my pajams, and in five minutes I looked very much like an old lady, out for the sights. My face was pale and slightly yellow after the previous night's entertainment, and I worked burnt match lines around my eyes in good old Psi U. theatrical style, and then in case of emergency, I had a veil.

"Molly was quick-witted and got me out of the Pequot the back way, and we hurried down to the wharf without any one suspecting me. But there, alas, (how I swore to myself!) we found the boat had gone! But, as luck would have it, one of Molly's school friends, with a lot of girls and Harvard men, whom we did n't know, were going to see the race on a private steam yacht, and were waiting for their chaperons to come along from the hotel. Molly talked with her friend, and introduced me. I played *my* part of 'Charlie's Aunt' in great shape, and they asked me if I would be willing to chaperon the crowd? Well, *I* was willing, you can better believe! for it was late and I wanted to see the race the worst way.

"The Harvard men got us all in their launch as quickly as possible, and, by Jupiter Omnes! we got aboard the yacht and crowded on all steam and started off for New London just as the real chaperons,—the mothers of two of the lads,—put in an appearance on the Pequot wharf! They waved and waved and shouted, but not a whit did *we* care. We were n't going to put back. Young Graham of Harvard shouted ' Very sorry. Take the trolley!' and off *we* sped at a twenty-mile gait for up the river. I could n't ask for any better treatment than I received, and my sister Molly stuck close to me to help me out in case I got into any trouble. They gave me the most comfortable seat in the boat under an awning in the stern, and when I said the water was apt to make me ill, and asked for clam broth (There is nothing like clam broth after a bat, boys), the steward brought me some of the best I ever tasted. It went to the right spot, I can tell you! And on that I ate a few crackers and toyed with some *pâté de fois gras*, and the sea air and all revived my drooping spirits in great shape.

"'Was n't it lucky Aunt Sarah had a headache and could n't go!' whispered Molly, as we sped along past Fort Hale.

"'Yes, indeed, and was n't it lucky to get on this yacht?'

"Molly presented all the girls one by one. They were all good enough looking, were it not for the unpleasantly trying colored ribbons they wore. Several of them kissed me. Gad! Just what they did to 'Charlie's Aunt'! I said to myself. But I did n't enjoy it at all, because I was 'all of a tremmer,' as Caddy Wilson says, lest they should get on to my fake disguise. I pretended to be a little seasick, and retired to the cabin, and lay down and got away from them, and every one went up forward on the bow.

"'Steward,' I said, 'I feel the need of a little trifle of stimulant.'

"'Brandy, ma'am?' he asked respectfully.

"'N-no, make me a Manhattan cocktail.'

"'Oh, very well, ma'am,' he said rather surprised.

"He was more surprised when I asked him for a second; but he did n't peep!

"Then Molly came down and said, 'Aunt, dear, we are going under the bridge now, won't you come out on deck?'

"'I'm afraid of being indecorous,' I said, and she frowned at me.

"'I shall be delighted, my dear,' I said, and she whispered, ' Now, Will, *do* be careful! Don't begin to shout rah, rah, rah, when you catch sight of the crew, and don't offer to bet.'

"' Oh, trust *me*,' I laughed. 'I've seen "Charlie's Aunt" three times, and have acted on the Psi U. stage as the *ingénue* from Squashtown. Just get on to my curves!'

" Molly nearly had a fit!

"Well, I went out on deck, and they placed my chair in the bow, in the best possible place to see, and put a footstool under my feet. Fellows, I tried my best to be calm and easy, but the air, and the sight of the yachts, and the clam-broth, and the cocktails,—and the thundering excitement I always felt, and always shall feel, as a patriotic son of Eli, just before a race at New London—What chap can help giving a yell as the 'Varsity slips out across the river with that perfect, smooth, equal, beautiful stroke? and I know, for I' ve been there, they put on a little extra finish,—the pharisees, as they came into the line,——just as a thoroughbred race-horse will prance and dance, and feel the keen delight of it all, as he goes to the post. And there, boys, were four of my old crew—the Dwarf,—*how his muscles shone that day!*—Oh, the Dwarf is a whole crew just in himself: handsome as a picture, strong as an ox, calm and confident as—as a New Haven oyster! You *can't* lose with the Dwarf in the boat. And—for me to sit there in my aunt's dress and see him, and Sawyer, and Bliss, and Parrish,—four of my old crew, and *not* yell!—and not get up and let 'em know their old cox', Little Jack, was there with his eye on 'em! and with 'em just the same as if he was in the boat, and rooting for 'em—well, it was madness! Boys, the tears rolled down my cheeks, I was so excited, and I had to suppress it, and my sister said it was the bright sunlight and made me put up a parasol! And when she gave it to me she was trembling like a leaf.

"And then out came Harvard in very good style, too, and lined up alongside, and there was but a little delay, and then——*they were off!* Harvard jumped away with the lead, but it did n't last long, and Yale slowly walked up. Well, when Yale forged a foot or two ahead, I could stand it no longer. I jumped up on my chair and yelled, 'Yale,—Yale,—Yale,—Brekity Kex,—coax, coax,—got 'em again—got 'em again! Paraboloo,—Ya-ale!!' Then I sat down in a hurry, and you ought to have seen my Harvard friends! You know what a voice I've got, developed by coaching,—it reached across the river, and the Dwarf heard it and I could see his old jaws grin with delight, and you chaps on the 'moving grand stand' heard it and yelled back, and things became quiet again until the last quarter mile, for Yale was gaining every stroke, and it was another dead cinch!

"But consternation reigned on our yacht! Not only on account of the race, but on account of me. My sister said it was only a 'paroxysm,'—whatever that was—and she pinched my arm, pretending to soothe me, until I nearly yelled again! She pulled the shawl close around my neck, and stuck a hat-pin into me, and with it all I could see she was half frightened, half convulsed with laughter.

"'Your aunt seems quite disposed to give vent to her enthusiasm,' said Paton, the owner of the yacht, one of the Harvard men, to my sister. 'But I hope you will persuade her—as this is a Harvard yacht we would prefer not to encourage Yale.'

"'She has a nephew there now at Yale,' said Molly. 'He was coxswain of the crew two years ago. I suppose she feels unusual interest.' And Molly bit her lip.

"'I think I never heard such a shrill cry,' said another Harvard man; 'I fancy your aunt must have been in great pain.'

"'She has not been well for a long time,' said my sister, sadly.

"'Nothing serious?' asked another Harvard man.

"'I am sorry to say that we were obliged,—er—it is very embarrassing——a private asylum, you know.'

"'Oh, I'm very sorry.'

"Meanwhile I was rocking to and fro in my chair, my head bent down mostly to my knees with laughing, and pleased to death to see the crew half a mile or so in advance. I was meditating, too, on the character of my aunt, whether, being a confessed ex-lunatic, it would not be exactly becoming in me to give vent to a little more encouragement to the crew. On the whole, however, I realized that they were so far in advance that it could really make no difference, and subsided and watched the proceedings in silence.

"Our yacht, the *Fairy*, steamed along behind the crowded press boat and the referees' boat, and the yachts were booming their cannon, and Yale blue was everywhere, and every one aboard the *Fairy*, except my sister, who kept silent,—was saying, 'This is too monotonous!' And then we came up alongside of our crew, who were resting on their oars, just under the great railroad bridge, and a Harvard man leaned down and made my blood run cold by calmly whispering in my ear, 'Yell all you want to, Eli, we've a plan to "do" you up later, and you may as well have all the fun you can out of it now!'

"So I thanked him, and stood up, and yelled! I gave 'em the rebel yell, 'Whah-o-o-o-Yale!' three times, and I saw old Dwarf laugh with the rest of the crew, and the Harvard men who were on to me, looked solemn but pretended that they thought it all right—You see of course they did n't want their girls to know."

"Going back down the harbor to the Pequot, they set up a handsome lunch on board, and as I knew the jig was up and something bad was in store for me [*I did n't tell my sister this,*] I allowed myself plenty of fizz, to quiet my nerves. Then you know my failing;—I began to get garrulous and talkative, and talked out everything I had in my head, and coming from a queer old lady, it must have seemed ridiculous to those girls. I heard one of them,—a Boston beaut—confide in a friend that she had never seen such a 'crazy old fright' in her life. Here's a specimen of a few of the silly things I remember I said in my character of chaperon!

"'Just leave me enough fizz, girls, and you can have just as good a time as you want. You can't shock *me* with anything you do.'

"You ought to have seen the indignation with which the Boston girl drew herself up after that!

"'I am sure she is nothing but a disgusting, vulgar creature,' I heard her say.

"'The Yale crew knew how to row and you did n't,' I said to a Harvard man. 'And the reason is they never use foreign champageny water.'

"The Harvard man expressed polite acquiescence, and turned away. So I tried to talk to the girls.

"'Girls,' I said, 'when I was at Vassar, I was on the crew,—and we had a hummer. I think we made a mile in ten minutes. We used to race the Hudson River boats. Lots of fun!'

"The girls looked at me more in sorrow than in anger. They believed I was deranged!

"When they got back to the Pequot, as I was the last one to step into the launch, to go ashore,—Gad! a Harvard man quietly gave me a sudden jerk, and over I went, head first into the water. My sister gave a scream, but they pretended they did n't notice anything, and the naphtha launch sputtered off ashore leaving me to clamber up the shiny white sides of the *Fairy*, swim ashore, or go down and see the oysters below. The sailors aboard the yacht looked over the side and grinned at me. Indeed, I must have been a healthy looking object! My bonnet came off in the water and, with a curse at them for not throwing me a rope, off I started for shore, and it happened the nearest shore was the Fort Griswold or Eastern side. But at the moment I did n't care much what shore it was, provided it was *shore.* I was used to the water, but it was deuced cold out there at the mouth of the harbor, and the waves were pretty high, too. I was glad enough to hear a familiar voice call out to me, after a few minutes swim, 'Hello, Jack, is that you?' It was Boots Paige and a lot of people on the *Osprey*, and they picked me up.

"They said. 'Well, where in thunder did you come from? And what in creation are you doing in that rig?'

"I told them I was out for a swim in a hired bathing suit, and—you'd laugh—they thought it was all right! You see, when my aunt's dress got soaked in the water, it looked very much like an old bathing dress, and every one was so excited over the race it made little difference.

"Well, they put me ashore at the Pequot and I sneaked around and got in through the back of the hotel and slipped up to my room and got into bed, for I didn't know exactly what else to do—and waited for something to happen!

"Presently, I heard a thundering knocking and I threw my wet dress under the bed and pretended to be asleep. Then Stoughton and Holworthy burst in on me, and Hol. said, ' He 's been asleep all through the race,—the d——d little fool!'

" ' It was a confounded low trick,' said Stoughton. 'Let 's wake him up and tell him Harvard won,—and then give him a d—d good dinner to pay for it.'

" So they shook me, and I woke up slowly and rubbed my eyes.

" ' Is it time to get up, fellows?' I asked.

" ' Pretty near,' said Holworthy, laughing, and fetching in my clothes on the quiet from his trunk, where he 'd locked 'em up.'

" ' Why, it 's late!' I gasped, springing out of bed. 'You 're all dressed! What a time we had last night,—I must have slept like a log!'

" I hurriedly dressed myself and kept talking about the race, and the ' sure thing' Harvard had, and giving them the biggest sort of a bluff to bet with me. But they seemed sort of low-spirited, and finally Holworthy said, ' I feel just as if the whole thing was over and Yale had won the race,—as usual.'

" ' So do I,' groaned Stoughton yawning.

"'Now, I'll tell you what I'll do,' I said, 'I don't see how we can win;—I understand one of our men has a felon on his hand——'

"'Your whole crew is a set of felons!' laughed Holworthy, dismally.

"'Then our boat is warped way out of shape,' I said. 'And they say it's cranky. I don't see how we can have the ghost of a show. Whereas it's a beauty—the Harvard crew.'

"Stoughton made a wry face. It was nuts to me to rub it in!

"'The Harvard crew is acknowledged by every one to be the best the Crimson has had for ten years. Of course, I expect to give odds. How would five to one suit you?

"Stoughton thought the odds fair, but 'did n't know.'

"'Well, I'll give you a hundred to twenty Yale wins the race!—Even the most died-in-the-wool Harvard man on earth *must*, for the sake of his college, accept *such* odds.'

"'I'm not betting this year,' yawned Holworthy.

"'Well, I'll bet you two hundred to twenty, Stoughton, Yale wins the race this year. Come now!'

"Stoughton said, 'Make that twenty dollars to two, and I don't mind,—for the honor of the old college,' and he winked at Holworthy.

"'Well,—I'll bet five hundred to ten.'

"'Those appear to be decent odds,' said Stoughton; 'but—you see—'

"'What odds does Harvard want this year?' I asked, pretending to be amazed.

"'Well,' said Stoughton, 'we think five hundred to a good cigar is about right!'

"And they both laughed.

"Then, as I was brushing my hair,—I felt fine as a fiddle after my bath,—they made an excuse and went down, to obtain something to cheer them in defeat, I suppose.

"I went down-stairs and met my sister, who told me she was relieved to see me skimming along the outer edge of the bathing houses, and so on up to my room, after last seeing me swimming about in the water. I explained how Holworthy and Stoughton had hid my clothes, and she asked:

"'How can you pay them off?'

"'I'll attend to them later. Meanwhile, I will try and get even with our Harvard friends aboard the *Fairy*.'

"'Oh,—they 've just invited a large party to go out for a 'tea and a sail,' she said, 'and have n't asked *us!*'

"'Very good,' I replied, and I sat down and wrote a note to the mate on a sheet of hotel paper, and signed it 'J. L. Paton,'—one of the owners. I sent this down to the wharf, where the mate was waiting with the launch,—by a hotel boy in buttons, and gave him a quarter to go on the dead run. Then my sister and I sauntered out on the piazza, and congratulated a lot of Yale people, and in a few minutes had the pleasure of seeing the *Fairy* crowd on all steam and head up the harbor!

"Paton and his Harvard friends,—there must have been twenty-five people,—a lot of stunning girls, too,—must have been somewhat surprised! I sent an order to the *Fairy* to steam at once up to Red Top, Harvard's quarters, four miles up the river, and wait there until Paton and party arrived!

"They all got down on the wharf in time to see the yacht steam off in great shape! Paton was in a regular blue funk! The mate, of course, thought they had concluded to go up in carriages.

"And how did you get even with Holworthy?"

"Never did. They gave me a great dinner and all that; but really, I had no grudge against those chaps, whatever. I'd had a good time, — saw the race under very pleasant circumstances, — and why, there you are!"

"But one thing, — what did your aunt say to it all?"

"Oh, she had just sat out there all day at the Pequot, looking on. 'I have had all the racing *I* needed,' she said, 'watching the students and their girl friends racing up and down the piazza!'"

AN HYPNOTIC SEANCE.

At the Barrington's, one night in August, the following proceedings took place, as narrated by Billy Scot, over several mugs of beer, in his room in Lawrance, to a number of fellows gathered there, and after he had made them an excellent rarebit, and set up some capital *pâté de fois gras*.

The story was told *à propos* of a certain learned Professor Dribble, (mathematics) who had just conditioned "Little Jack" Horner in Conic Sections, and against whom poor Little Jack had been humorously (and otherwise) animadverting all the evening, in more or less terse and emphatic language.

"To ease your mind, Jack," said Scot, "I'll tell you of the grind on 'Drib,' which we played on him down at Sands Point, last August. He isn't infallible,—and it's possible that he's made a mistake in your stand,—though you can't get him to admit it. He was there at the hotel with his solemn wife and son, and, as he knew old Mr. Barrington, he came over to call one evening. We found him there when we all got back from sailing. There were "Great's" three sisters, a Miss Standish,—a beaut— a Miss Hallows, of New York, and "Boots" Paige, Great, and myself;—Oh! I forgot Mrs. Barrington, who is the champion chaperon of America,—deaf and not inclined to talk, and a great sleeper. She holds the state record of engagements of couples directly under her charge. I forget how many,—twenty-seven, I think. Well, we got back and found the Professor there, and Great and I thought it was an excellent opportunity to get even for several past little amenities,—he and I never got on well since he forced me to hand him up a paper I happened to have in my hand, at the board, one day in Freshman year. He was so certain *sure* it was a skinning paper! I gave it to him, and,—poor old chap,—he had to read this wretched doggerel:

> "There was an old prof, named Dribble,
> Who taught us to cipher and scribble,
>   We know that he drinks
>   Ice water and thinks
> As a psychical crank—He's a dibble!

"He is an hypnotic crank, you know, and he tried to hypnotize me after recitation that day when he called me up;—but I pretended I did n't know what was on the paper and that I 'd just picked it up from the floor, and he did n't get on to what was going on in my mind. 'Nay, nay—Pauline!' If he had, he 'd been more disgusted than ever!

"Well, *revenons à nos muttons*, as they say in Paree. We went in and introduced him all around to all the girls and coached Miss Leila Barrington to ask him if he was not a member of the Boston Society of Psychical Research? and to say that she had often heard of his hypnotic power. She asked on her own account, would he use his strange power to compel a favorable or an unfavorable answer to a question in class room? He answered, I remember his exact words, ' I try to be absolutely and strictly impartial in the class room, Miss Leila—'"

"*He* impartial! every one knows the old fellow has his favorites, and does his best to help them over hard places!" put in Little Jack.

"'Of course, *generally!*' said Miss Leila. Awfully clever girl, Leila Barrington.

An Hypnotic Seance. 233

"'But, if a student was very low in his stand, would you not hypnotize him into giving the right answer, to help him out? Say he was near being dropped for low stand?'

"'Well, hardly,—I should hope not!'

"'Professor, I think you *might*—' she said.

"'No, not on your life you would n't!' sang out Boots Paige, after which there was a little pause,—in fact, a dead silence.

"'Professor Dribble,' said Great, 'we all have a great interest in mind reading, and hypnotism. We tried an experiment the other morning, and owing to the wonderful talent of Miss Standish, (here Miss Standish giggled) we precipitated a really remarkable case of mind transference, telepathy you call it, do you not?'

"'Ah, indeed?' asked Professor Dribble, stroking his grizzle beard, and very much interested. 'Yes, we call some instances telepathy.'

"'Suppose we repeat the experiment now,' I said, 'for the professor's benefit.'

"The girls, not knowing exactly what we were going to do, gave a grudging sort of assent, fearing that the professor would discover the joke.

"'Would you like to have the experiment tried?' asked Miss Leila, going up to the professor very demurely.

"'Oh, very much,—yes, indeed. Anything new is just so far an addition to our human knowledge on this occult subject. Really, it will gratify me very much.'

"'Well then, Professor, will you go out into the hall, and I will close the door,' I said, at the same time cautioning him not to listen. 'You won't try to deceive us, will you?'

"'Certainly not!' he said, and out he went.

"When the door was shut, the girls were all in a panic. They were afraid of him, you see. He looked very fierce and earnest.

"'Why, he's easy fruit,' said Great, laughing.

"'Now, then, I'll call him in and tell him that we will join hands, and he must take yours, Miss Standish, for I told him and he believes you are the arch high-priestess of witch-craft among us, and full of electricity.'

"'Oh, I'm too frightened!' she exclaimed, laughing.

"'Why, it's nothing. Let me explain. It's an old gag. We'll all sit down in a circle, holding hands; the professor will come in. We are supposed to choose a word, anything, and he is supposed to read it through our hands, —see? Now, I will say to him, 'Speak out, Professor, the first phrase or word that distinctly occurs to your mind.' Then suppose he says the word 'Senegambia,' we must all give a shout, and say 'that's it! that's it!' After he has done it once or twice, I'll go out and then you must really choose a word,—see? and Miss Leila, you must spell it out with your finger on my wrist, as you hold my hand; one for A, two for B, three for C, and so forth down the alphabet; and then I'll say it out and you must shout as before. See?'

"'Yes,' said Miss Leila, 'we see, of course, but that mind-reading joke is awfully stale,—it's been played for ever so long; it was a regular game at Bar Harbor last summer.'

"'I don't believe the professor has ever been horsed by it,' said Great, 'Let's try it on anyway.'

"'Why, we sold everybody we could with that at Nantucket years ago,' said one of the Barrington girls. 'Of course he will know it.'

"'Well, we've got him out of the room now, and *must* do something with him,' said I.

"'Oh, Mr. Scot, why not let him hypnotize you?' said Miss Leila.

"'No, he might order me to kiss every girl in the room, and that would be too embarrassing!' and Scotty pretended to blush.

"'Oh, let's try it on anyway!' said Great. 'Perhaps he won't know the trick; he may never have seen it.'

"So, after a good deal of discussion the circle was formed and the professor brought in.

"It was very evident that he had not seen the trick (common enough—Heaven knows!) played before. Boots turned down the gas to a dim religious light and turned out the lamps, and we all sat in solemn silence fully five minutes.

"'Really,' said the professor, 'I don't feel like pronouncing anything.'

"'Think now, concentrate your mind,' said Boots,—using the professor's usual dicta of the class room.

"Then Professor Dribble smirked and smiled with sudden great joy and came out with '*Aliquando bonus dormitat Homerus!*'

"'Yes! That's it! that's it!'—as if those poor girls could remember a Latin sentence for five minutes!

"The professor said, 'Oh, I'm not at all astonished, the atmospheric conditions seem favorable; I congratulate you, Miss Standish, you have a most delicate and unusual nervous sense; I could feel the electric current distinctly. Your hand-pressure is exceedingly delicate —but firm——'

"Barrington said, 'Yes—she had a firm grasp of the subject!'

"Miss Standish, who was a stunning pretty girl, laughed and blushed, and we all said, 'Oh —oh—oh! however could you do it!' and the girls made faces at her—to her confusion.

"You see, the Professor had long been a believer in and a supporter of the most advanced theories of hypnotism and mind transference, and everything went with him in great shape. He was quite *ready* to believe, which I understand is a necessary condition to be in, in all of these occult mysteries. He was ready to believe anything, for the old well-worn trick had never been played on him before.

"The girls laughed and giggled and enjoyed it immensely, and old Mr. Barrington came in and we told him the joke, and he laughed louder than the rest, and the professor never caught on. We went in and horsed him to his bent.

"He went out of the room again and this time he announced the phrase 'Enthusiasm is a waste of energy,' and we all waved our handkerchiefs and shouted as before. The professor was quite carried away, and took careful notes of all that happened.

"Then I think, Paige went out, and Boots acted the thing up in great shape. He seemed to go into a trance and rolled up his eyes and called out, 'Mother, where are you?' twice, and made all sorts of grimaces, and kept us in roars of laughter, and then announced the word 'Humbug!' which was the word Leila and her brother had selected.

"Then Great went out and came in and announced 'Professor,' a word which he had selected, of course;—then he went out and came in again and announced 'Badly Fooled.'

"We thought *sure* he would catch on to this but he did n't, he was so taken up with the perfect thought-transfer that was taking place. You see he was n't thinking of anything else. Poor old chap!

"Then we tried the *Ouija* game on him, and

horsed him quite as badly in that. Oh, it was great! Drib was completely taken in, and we were glad to have him get out of the house without some of the girls giving it away. The elder Miss Barrington began to show great compunction, and we had to 'work it' to get him away."

"How did you accomplish that?"

"Very simply. Great slipped off down cellar and turned off all the gas, and I got Drib's hat and cane and gently led him out, and bade him good evening."

"That was certainly a very *gentle* hint!"

"Well,—you have to 'hammer' old Drib!" and Scot laughed.

"And that is the last you've heard of it?"

"Yes,—except for the copy of the *Psychic Science Review*, in which the Professor's account of what transpired that evening is most accurately set down. It is marked Case 112, 896. We bought a dozen copies and sent them to all the girls."

Billy Scot took the *Review* out of his inside pocket, and read aloud from the professor's paper:

"Case No. 112, 896, in the *Psychic Science Review*.

"On the eighteenth day of August, 189-, while making a social visit on John B. Barrington, Esq., and lady, at his country seat, at Sands Point, Ct., the following actual occurrences took place:

"I was invited by Mr. P., a student at Yale, to join my right hand to that of a young lady, Miss S., and my left to that of Miss B. A circle was then formed consisting of eight persons, who had previously and while I was out of the room with the door shut, selected a phrase which was to be communicated to me solely by manual touch.

"We had been sitting in a chain for four minutes, thirty-two seconds, when the phrase, '*Aliquando bonus dormitat Homerus*,' forced itself from my lips. It transpired that *this was the very phrase that was selected*. I wish to call especial attention to the facts, (1) that the phrase was in the Latin tongue, (2) that no other or secondary phrase was suggested, (3) that it being the first test, more time was consumed than in the subsequent experiments for the induction of the suggestion, (4) that no fascina-

An Hypnotic Seance.   241

tion, which plays an important part in hypnosis, was exercised on me by either lady, (5) that in no way was hypnosis induced by means of the eye.

"The next experiment resulted in my announcing the sentence, ' Enthusiasm is a waste of energy,' which was correct.

"During the induction of this sentence, which required two minutes, thirty-six seconds, I inadvertently pressed the hand of Miss S., who hastily withdrew her hand from mine, and again resumed connection with me only on the earnest entreaty of all present. I attributed my sudden pressure to animal magnetism, and so stated at the conclusion of the test, but this seemed to be disbelieved by those present."

"A third test was then made, I announcing correctly 'Cross as two sticks,' in a little less than two minutes.

"Another gentleman, Mr. P., then left the room, and in his absence we selected the word 'Humbug.'

"Mr. P., on making one of the circle, exhibited at once the extraordinary phenomena of hypnosis. The lids of his eyes half closed, his eyeballs turned up, exhibiting to those in the room only the whites. His head fell back, and then upon his left shoulder. After one minute and forty-three seconds, he emitted groans of a dismal character and breathed heavily. He then announced the word 'Hum,' paused for three minutes, and then announced the word 'bug.' On breaking the chain, Mr. P. came completely to himself, but was heard to complain of the heat and to ask for his maternal parent. The temperature of the room being (without accurate measurement) about 84° Fahr.

"Young Mr. B., then, without manifestations of extraordinary hypnosis, after two minutes, thirty-three seconds, announced the word 'Professor,' and afterwards, after three minutes, four seconds, the two words 'Badly fooled.'

"All of which I subscribe to, and desire to bear witness to, over my signature and notarial certificate, which see below.

"A desire for experimentalization in thought transference on planchette, or, what is the same toy, *Ouija*, being expressed, a board was promptly placed on the table, in the centre of the room.

"Miss S. seated herself at the board and

An Hypnotic Seance.

placed her hands upon the planchette. Mr. P. sat opposite, and placed one hand on the board. Certain questions were asked by Miss B., who stood at the further end of the room, her back turned.

"Question 1. Of whom am I thinking?

"Answer by *Ouija:* Tommy Atkyns.

"Miss B. admitted this to be the correct if remarkable answer.

"Question 2. Of whom am I thinking now?

"Answer. A handsome man.

"Question 3. What does he look like?

"Answer. A bearded chimpanzee.

"Question 4. What is his name?

"Answer. Professor Dribble.

"On Miss B. stating that the answer was incorrect, *Ouija* answered, 'Sometimes called Fribble.'

"As this was the first incorrect answer of the evening, it was determined to ask in a further attempt.

"Question 5. Is the spirit of George Washington present?

"Answer. Yes.

"Question 6. Will he speak through *Ouija?*

"Answer. Perhaps.

"Question 7. Why perhaps?

"Answer. The lady is not entirely truthful.

"Miss S. at this point abruptly retired, and Miss Leila B., a sister of the interlocutor, took her seat at the table.

"Question 8. Will he speak now?

"Answer. Certainly.

"Question 9. How old would you be if you were now living, George?

"Answer. Almost old enough to be your grandpa, dear.

"Question 10. Are you happy where you are?

"Answer. Of course. There are no marriages in heaven.

"Of course these answers naturally afforded the guests assembled considerable diversion and amusement. The answers demonstrated the peculiar playfulness of those in the Spirit world. This has been often remarked before. The interrogation of Washington continued for some time in the same light vein, and then the following questions were put:

"Question 11. If not yourself, who would you rather be?

"Answer. Professor Dribble.

"Question 12. Why?

"Answer. Because he is a medium.

"Question 13. You mean he has extraordinary powers?

"Answer. Extraordinary mental powers, with one defect.

"Question 14. What is that?

"Answer. He can't see through a mill-stone with a hole in it.

"Question 15. You mean he is not clairvoyant?

"Answer. Opaque.

"Question 16. What must he do to be clairvoyant?

"Answer. Eat isinglass.

"Question 17. And what else?

"Answer. Go west.

"This was most extraordinary, as I had only the previous week received a call to the chair of higher mathematics at Oberlin, over which I was then debating, but since which time I have declined.

"At this point, Miss Leila B. rose from the table, stating that it 'made her tired,'[1] and the

---

[1] Often the case with hypnotic subjects owing to neural disturbance.—H. R. D.

experimentation ceased, at ten hours, fourteen minutes. Shortly after I returned to my hotel, and immediately made the above memoranda of facts. It is only by an accumulation of evidence such as the foregoing, that we shall in time, in my judgment, arrive at the true scientific basis of thought transference, or telepathy.

"With great respect, I am,
"Yours,
"HENRY R. DRIBBLE.

"State of Conn. }
County of Blank. } ss.

"HENRY R. DRIBBLE, being duly sworn, makes oath this 19th day of August, 1891, and says that the above account is in substance strictly true.
"J. R. JONES,
"Notary Public, Blank County. Ct."

A VIOLENT REMEDY.

SUSCEPTIBLE Adolphus Austin, during the long vacation of the previous summer, had met at Bar Harbor, and afterwards followed to the mountains, a certain Miss Fanny Gower, who from all accounts, was not bad. Paige, who had met her, said she was nice people. "Sleuth" Davidson, who was a great judge, knew her, too, and said he never cared for those impassive summer creatures who look down on a man from such a tremendous height,—and expect you to keep them in candy and reading matter and flowers, and who always were on the make, —and expected you to pay for being with them at so much an hour, in carriage and boat hire. "I give that class the shake," said Sleuth, of the level head, "and let them understand at once that I am the only son of an aged widow, who supports me!"

Adolphus had followed his inamorata down from Mt. Desert to the Profile House, and had danced and flirted with her all through August and September, and just before his return to College, on a coaching party through the mountains, had been gently but distinctly informed that she could only hold to him the position of a devoted sister. He acquiesced in her decision but it had "knocked him silly" as they said. He had been harder hit than he imagined, and when he got back to the Eveless paradise of Welch Hall, he fell into a gentle melancholy over his affair which showed no signs of yielding to the exquisitely humorous chaffing of his chum and their friends.

He was a good fellow,—and the girl, of course, had treated him shamefully,—so they said; and he ought to be glad to give up such a cruel-hearted flirt and whistle her down the winds, etc. With the "crowd," any girl who had been at all "repellent" was an arch flirt.

"She's been an angel,—a perfect angel," he said; "and I don't deserve her, and it was only her goodness of heart which prompted her to let me remain near her as long as I did."

"Spending twenty dollars a day for her amusement,—" interlarded "Laze" Aldrich, his chum, over his briarwood.

Austin only sighed.

"And when, like an ass, I went too far,—and told her how impossible it was to exist without her——"

"The season being over, and she being on the point of going back to town——"

"She kindly told me that she could not possibly bring herself seriously to care for me, and that we must part forever."

"Well,—Adolphus,—don't take it too much to heart; there are others."

"There is but one Fanny Gower!"

Then Austin threw himself into a deep easy chair and lit his pipe.

"My advice is, always let the girl fall in love with *you;* not you with the girl," said Aldrich sententiously.

"Well,—it's all over now," sighed Adolphus. "I shall never marry, Laze. I'm over all that sort of thing now, for all time, and yet,—I dreamed——"

Austin looked gloomily out of the window.

Aldrich sniffed, and burst out:

"Poor old idealist! Don't you know that all girls are selfish, vain, merely imitative creatures, and affected? If you don't,—why—I'm deuced sorry for you."

"Aldrich, you 're a cynic. Most girls have a wider, more spiritual and higher view of life than we men are capable of."

Aldrich turned to his *Jevon's Logic* impatiently.

Then Adolphus sat down at the piano and began to sing softly:

> "I shot an arrow into the air,
> It fell to earth,—I know not where——"

Aldrich rudely interrupted, in a hoarse basso:

> "The next day a man came round
> And sold me a dead dog at a dollar a pound——"

—It was n't original with Aldrich, he got it out of a newspaper, but he liked to sit on his chum's manifestations of sentiment as often and as severely as he could. To be afflicted with sentiment he deemed "dreadfully effeminate," and Austin was getting to be too sentimental for any living with him.

He went up to see Keith and Horner in Lawrance, after a little while, and said, as he entered the room: "Damn a lovesick fool!"

"Why?"

"My chum——"

"Adolphus?—still stuck on that pretty Fanny Gower? Why, she 's a wicked flirt!"

Little Jack threw his book down and cocked his feet up on a table, and lit a cigarette.

"Yes,—just a nice tidy little flirt,—that's all," said Aldrich, half provoked, half laughing, "but she's spoiled *him*."

Little Jack Horner puffed at his cigarette thoughtfully.

"There's only one way to cure a lovesick fool," he said solemnly. "Get him to fall in love with a new girl." He puffed twice again. "Then, when he's fallen *out* with the new girl, he's cured—See?"

"Well, where's your new girl?"

"Oh, any girl will do, I suppose,"

"Now, that seems to me rattling good sense."

"I mean,—if you can't find one,—make up one.'

"That's even more sensible!"

"Oh, Tom Keith," called Little Jack, "Come in here!"

At the moment Tom Keith was in his bedroom trying on his make-up for the joint-play (Psi U and D.K.E.) and as he was cast for a fashionable daughter of a tremendously rich banker, his sudden apparition at the door astonished Aldrich to a degree. Keith made the prettiest girl in college by all odds. His oval face, straight features, clear blue eyes and nicely pencilled eyebrows, and small hands and feet, gave him enormous advantages. He was the college soubrette *par excellence.*

"My boy—I mean girl—you are a winner! I'd never know you!" exclaimed Aldrich, in admiration. "If you *were* one, now, I'd have to speak to your father!"

Keith adjusted his blond wig before the glass. Then he adjusted his large hat on the wig, and whitened his face with a powder-puff. Several fellows dropped in and made comments, complimentary and otherwise. Keith began to put on airs.

"How about your voice, Tom?"

"Oh, I sha'n't mind about that,—lots of girls have regular boys' voices, you know.—And I've heard that nowadays to talk way down in their boots, like men, was just the cheese."

Keith, satisfied that his gown would fit, began to disrobe.

"Say,—Tom,—er—er—don't—before us!— what do you say to having a little sport out of Adolphus!" and Little Jack Horner puffed out a cloud of smoke. " He's lovesick, you know, all girled up. It's our duty to get him out of it."

" How ? "

" Put on your sacque and go over and pretend to want to see Aldrich, and say you will wait for him to return; Austin is there. Be rather reserved at first,—try it,—and don't let him find out who you are."

" What the deuce shall I talk about ? "

" Oh,—say you're a cousin of Laze,—and that you are down from school for a few days —you can work it as you see he bites or not. Talk as seriously as you can about life, and the future, and throw in a little religion. You know Adolphus pretty well,—you know his soft spots."

" Yes,—and you might hint at having a broken heart about you," said Aldrich.

" Adolphus is in a sentimental mood just now over that Gower girl,—she's thrown him down ; it would be a kindness to him to flirt a little with him. If he bites, all right,—get him out of his doldrums, if you can. He's been moping the last month."

" After half an hour or so, Laze will go back,"

said Jack, "and be so surprised to see his cousin 'Bessie,' and introduce you—Then you'd better make some excuse, Laze, and get out again. And, Tom, you make an appointment to-night, late, after your rehearsal, with Austin, if you can, and take a moonlight drive with him."

"I'm willing,—if we can make it go all right," said Keith. "But you must all stand by me."

"Oh, we'll take care of that!—we'll set him up a dinner afterwards;—a dinner always straightens everything out, you know."

So after a little, Keith,—now to be known as Miss Bessie Aldrich, just from school, slipped out of the room, and so over to north entry, Welch, up two flights, and knocked timidly at Austin and Aldrich's door.

"Come in," sang out Austin in a loud voice, concluding from the gentle knock that it was his washerwoman.

The door opened, and Bessie entered; Adolphus who was seated with his back to the door, over a long pipe in a deep-bottomed easy chair, did not turn to look at her.

"Just lay it down anywhere, Mrs. Gimly,—

and I'll pay you when you call Saturday. Owe you for last week, don't I? By the way, you always seem, most lamentably, to exhaust all your starch, intended, no doubt, for my collars and shirts, in my towels and underclothing. Now, I do not care to have my silk socks starched particularly, and the towels are better as they are. And—d——n it—you really have very little sense, for so advanced a person, Mrs. Gimly, and you seem to think I have a 16 neck —my number is $14\frac{1}{2}$ you know,——By Jove! —I—I—beg your pardon!"

Bessie exclaimed in a high key, "Sir—you have apparently no idea who I am!"

Adolphus had glanced up, and caught sight of the pretty blonde, who appeared to be extremely shocked at his highly unparliamentary language. He bounced out of his easy chair, and proceeded to make a dozen apologies at once.

"Is my cousin, Mr. Aldrich in?" Bessie asked timidly as he finished.

"No,—not at present. He stepped out a moment ago. Won't you be seated and wait for him? he'll be back presently."

"Thanks," seating herself on the edge of a

chair. "I—I came down from school to see Cousin Dick, and—I'm to be in New Haven a few days."

"Oh, that's very good of you, and my chum will be delighted to see you,—I'm sure—I—I did n't know he had a cousin at school."

Austin stood, half leaning on the cushioned window seat, and Bessie drew herself as much as possible into the shadow of the curtain, out of the light. So far, he had bitten very well.

"I know it must seem dreadful to come right up to his room this way, without sending word,—but,—I—I am alone."

"Oh, I'm sure you have done just the right thing."

"I'm afraid Cousin Dick will think I'm awfully forward."

"Why,—not at all!"

"You see,—I—I have never been in New Haven before, and I am so frightened—I have n't any chaperon."

Bessie's eyes dropped modestly.

"I assure you a chaperon is usually a great bore—when awake. She is generally in the way,—and among college men is considered entirely unnecessary under any circumstances."

Adolphus stared at the pretty bit of femininity with all his might. She did n't smile. She seemed so timid, so remote, that he at once assumed a fatherly, protecting air.

"It might have been better to telegraph your arrival," he said. "If you will wait,—I will go and try to find your cousin."

"Oh, no—don't go, please."

"Oh, very well."

"I 've heard so much about you, Mr. Austin, from Cousin Dick—he has told me how bright you are,—and h—how you despise girls."

"I, despise girls? I may not approve of girls—but I do *not* despise them!" And Adolphus beamed compassionately upon her.

Then Bessie giggled.

"I 'm such a little goose!—I 'm afraid to be left alone."

Austin glanced quickly at Bessie, and the latter bit her lip, feeling that she had gone too far.

"Er—er—is this your first visit to New Haven?"

"Yes."

"I hope it won't be your last."

"Thank you, sir."

"Suppose I put on my hat and while we wait for my chum,—suppose I show you around the buildings. The windows in the library are considered quite good——"

"Oh, let us wait for Cousin Dick." She glanced quickly, half coquettishly at him, and he quickly recognized the fact that she was pretty, and that she demanded from him the admiration due a pretty girl.

Bessie kept putting her handkerchief to her lips in an odd sort of way, and half hiding herself behind the curtain. It was difficult for him to judge of her face,—to decide that she was a blown beauty,—he could only judge so from the furtive side glances she gave him.

Then there came a knock at the door, and Bessie gave a little scream, and said: "Oh, I am *so* frightened! I'll just step in here, if I may,—and close the door."

So in she went, into Aldrich's bedroom.

Austin opened the door, and in came Tutor Blinky, looking quite solemn. He closed the door behind him softly and said .

"Mr. Austin,—I happened to be coming in the entry and observed a young lady enter your room. Of course it is all right and proper but after a little consideration, I determined to speak to you about it; the College rules forbid the presence of a lady, unaccompanied by a chaperon, in the dormitories. I may point out to you——"

At that moment Laze Aldrich sauntered in.

"Oh,—Tutor Blinky,—delighted to see you."

"I was just saying that a female,—a young lady was seen entering your room." said the tutor.

"A young lady? Is she here now?" asked Aldrich.

"Of course, it's all right, but I merely wished to call attention to the rule——"

"But where is she?" Aldrich looked under the table, in his search.

"I don't *see* her," said the Tutor, rubbing his hands together, nervously.

"Then she's gone?"

"No,—she has n't gone!" Austin conveyed to his chum.

"She may be in that room," said the Tutor, indicating Aldrich's bedroom.

Aldrich walked over to the closed door of the room and said in a loud voice, "Tutor

Blinky, you must be mistaken, you will find no one in the room."

Then he waited a slight interval, and opened the door. The room was empty.

As the Tutor (of a notoriously spying disposition) could see plainly into Austin's room also, he concluded that the young lady had left, and said so.

Austin said firmly, "No young lady has passed *out* of this door, sir, I assure you. Yes, —I am positive!"

"No young woman has been here at all," said Aldrich positively, and perhaps a little rudely.

The Tutor bowed, looked crestfallen, and took his departure. "Very likely I was mistaken," he said, as he bowed himself out.

"Well!" exclaimed Austin. "Your cousin *was* here,—and she went into your room on hearing Tutor Blinky knock. But where she is *now*,—it's a mystery!"

"Why, Austin, my dear boy, you are dreaming! The only cousin I have is at school, up at Hartford."

"But she was here,—in that chair,—only a few minutes ago. Very pretty girl, too."

"I think you've got all girled up over that Miss Gower,—you have them on the brain! If my cousin (who by the way is quite an heiress, Adolphus) was here, why isn't she here now? She was quite a substantial young lady the last time I saw her."

"She is still,—she's very easy people. By Jove,—she couldn't have got out of my window, of course,—but, where is she?"

"Poor old chap! you have had an hallucination, as they call it. Describe her. If you've been asleep and dreamed of Cousin Bessie, it's a strange thing, but it's happened before to people."

"It is true I was *almost* asleep when she came in,—and first thought she was my washerwoman."

"The whole thing has been a hypnotic suggestion. You never saw my cousin *really*, you saw a *projection* of her, as they call it. She must be coming down to see me—I dare say I shall receive a telegram any moment."

Presently in came a number of fellows, and later on Keith in his ordinary clothes entered. And Austin, in the fulness of his heart, told them about the beautiful apparition, enlarging upon her beauty and style until they could with difficulty keep from laughing.

"It's because you are so hipped on a girl you think you see one behind every bush!" laughed his chum. "I believe you're going crazy."

"But Tutor Blinky saw her!"

"He must have seen my aunt and cousin who came up to see me just that very moment," promptly spoke up Johnson, who was in the plot, and who roomed in the same entry. They all agreed that Austin had had a strange hallucination and his chum suggested that he have a doctor at once.

Then, a few moments later, a messenger boy brought a telegram which read:

"Richard B. Aldrich, Yale College.
"Will be down on the evening train. Please meet me.
"Bessie."

"Well," said Aldrich. That *is* strange! She has "projected" herself into your mind, Billy! "The telegram is dated Hartford. At all events, we'll find out to-night if she has been here this afternoon,—and of course, she has n't. You have heard me speak of her a good many times?—what a splendid girl she is, and all that, and I've told her of you, and perhaps she thought of you and me to-day,—see? You can ask her when she comes if she was thinking of you about three o'clock. It's quite a mystery,—but people who believe in telepathy and that sort of thing say it's commoner than is supposed."

It was odd how every one else in the room concurred in what Laze said. Austin began to doubt his own senses.

After they had all gone, and as they were preparing to go out to afternoon recitation, Austin said:

"It's queer I never had an hallucination about Fanny Gower, or Kate Flemming or the others."

"That's because they never cared for *you*."

"But Bessie——?"

"She's heard a good deal about you, Adolphus—I've told her a lot. Who knows but the dear girl has been cherishing your image in her secret heart! She saw your photo once at home, I remember,—and she said, 'That's a damn fine looking chum of yours,'—or words to that effect."

"I hope Bessie does n't swear!" exclaimed Austin astonished.

"Well, she used some sort of girl's lingo,—I think she really said, 'He looks like an opera tenor singer,'—that's *their* ideal, you know. Oh, she in her tender young heart has quietly learned a good deal about you, Adolphus,—and, I dare say——"

"What rot!"

"I dare say she has scribbled your name all over her Fasquelle,—as girls will,—you know it's a way they have!"

"Absurd!"

But it was evident that Adolphus was secretly very well pleased with the idea.

They walked over to the recitation room in silence,—Austin meditating upon the surprising events of the afternoon. Just before they entered, he said: "Forgive me, old man, but when she comes to-night, and you happen to speak of me,—I—I would n't say anything about the Gower matter,—eh?"

"No,—certainly not!"

"And,—do caution Miss Bessie on going about alone,—er—er—Very odd about her 'counterfeit presentment'—was n't it! I don't think I could have been asleep?"

And Aldrich gave him an understanding glance, as they entered recitation. "I see," he said, "you think if it was not a dream it was highly improper?"

"Oh, no—but—"

"Well I will see that she is properly chaperoned——"

Bessie duly arrived that night, was properly introduced to Austin, and for the week following met him by appointment each evening, and took the most entrancing moonlight drives with him and "Cousin Dick," explaining that she was visiting people in New Haven, who were dead opposed to romance and extremely strict, and who, in fact, forbade students the house. The affair had such a strange beginning for Austin, and was kept up under such odd, romantic circumstances, with such mysterious meetings, and Bessie showed so much feeling for him, (she had, however, not yet allowed him to kiss her) that his wicked chum was able to report that Fanny Gower's name had not been mentioned since the day of the apparition! The ingenuity of Little Jack Horner was exercised to invent all sorts of charming and fascinating stories about Bessie. How she had saved her aged grandfather from a burning fate, in a country house; how she once caught a burglar, and how she had saved many a poor little newsboy's life from a passing express wagon. Bessie herself so arranged and ordered it that at last he confessed he loved her, with an audience of four or five delighted Juniors in hiding. Poor Adolphus was fairly caught in the trap!

"But,—Mr. Austin,—I've heard,—a little bird has told me that there is another."

"You allude to Fanny Gower? I assure you, Bessie,—*that* affair is all over."

They stood together beneath a gas-lamp, on Whalley Avenue, where they had just alighted from their open phaeton.

"But I come to *you*,—Adolphus—without a 'first' affair."

"I know,—but really, I find I never cared for Fanny—it was a momentary,—a foolish episode. I repent of it,—deeply."

(Subdued applause behind a clump of trees!)

"You must wait. I can't say that you are altogether repugnant to me. I can't deny, dear, you have an awfully winning way!"

"*Dear* Bessie!"

"But on next Friday night,—I shall be at the Joint theatricals. Until then you must wait,—and not see me. I expect to be busy. Tell me that night if,—you—still love me,—and write me in the care of Cousin Dick every day."

"And you'll give me a kiss to remember you till then?—that's four days off, Bessie!"

"No! I never kissed a man in my life." And this of course was strictly true.

"Oh, Bessie!"

Austin grasped her in his arms and tried to kiss her, but received a powerful slap which sent him reeling. Then Bessie turned and walked rapidly off in the darkness. She was on her dignity.

"Gad!—what a muscle that girl has got!" exclaimed poor Adolphus, ruefully. "These modern athletic girls are—are easily capable of taking care of themselves!"

During the ensuing four days Austin was in despair.

The strict relatives were stricter than ever and Bessie could not be seen at all.

Aldrich told his chum that he was afraid Bessie, who, he said, had been most properly brought up, probably hated him on account of his impudence in asking her for a kiss. Adolphus wrote her two love-letters a day, (Aldrich kept these under lock and key and brought them out occasionally afterward to a roomful of fellows when Austin was not present) and more mawkish, foolish love-letters, no son of Eli ever wrote in his life. Here are a few specimens:

" Dearest Bessie : —

"Forgive me, darling, for being too loving. I fear you are of a cold, icy nature,—your heart only beats once every half hour. Let me tell you,—you don't begin to understand what a man is made of, etc. etc."

" DARLING BESSIE :—

"You are the only girl I could ever feel that I truly loved. The spirits had something to do with our first acquaintance,—and the gods on Olympus now call joyfully to one another and say, 'another mortal pair are made immortal.' My chum tells me that you have a headache to-day ;—do be careful about wet feet, won't you? etc., etc., . . . I long for Friday night to come,—and then I shall see you again. You,—you only shall I see! Will you be in a box? How I wish we could sit side by side.

ADOLPHUS."

Bessie's letters were full of repression and caution:

" MY DEAR ADOLPHUS: —

"You must try not to *over* love me. Go slow, old man. The first thing I know, you'll do yourself some injury. You're a terribly knowing young man,

—and the idea of wanting to kiss me on a public avenue! Oh, Adolphus! you must be more careful. You must reform. Are you sure you are through with that Gower girl? Don't you really care for her any longer? If you do, I shall never speak to you again, never, never!

"B.

"P.S. N.B. I shan't be in a box Friday night, but in a stew, you can believe, dear."

"DEAR ADOLPHUS:—

"Your last was a corker! As a lover, you are too over sure. You say you never cared for a girl before Fanny Gower,—I say you never have cared for one since! Be more circumspect;—don't write my name all over your text books. Remember, and see me Friday night.

"P.S. N.B. The next time you see me,—it won't be in a carriage,—but a stage!

"B."

It is needless to say that Adolphus wondered a great deal at these enigmatical and mystifying postscripts!

At last the night of the Joint play came around. The fashionable daughter of a tremendously rich banker, as the pretty girl of the piece, made a great hit in the comedy played, and no one in all the audience was hit harder than Austin, who, in evening dress, occupied a seat in the front row of the gallery.

"Why, they 've got a real girl—Bessie Aldrich—in the daughter's part!" he said, surprised, as she came on in the first act.

"Yes," said Little Jack Horner, next to him. "We had to call in a little outside talent."

" But it *says*, ' Belinda—T. W. Keith.' That's Tom Keith ! "

"Oh, that's a blind!" laughed Aldrich on the other side. " She did n't want to let *every* fool in the audience know she was n't a student."

"Oh, I see," said Adolphus, thoughtfully.

" Do you ? " laughed Little Jack Horner.

"So they got Bessie to act—Well! Is n't she lovely ! Why did n't she tell *me* ? "

" Kept it as a surprise," said Aldrich.

"Oh—I see!" said Austin slowly, and then he added : " By—Jehoshaphat ! Jinks ! "

Adolphus Austin fastened his eyes on the beautiful daughter of the rich banker in apparently utter entrancement. At the first intermission, he hastened out, was gone some time and brought in with him a huge bouquet of flowers. He then fastened his card on the handle, and threw it full at Bessie, when she came on the stage, in the second act.

The bouquet struck her full in the chest and floored her. It was flung as hard as an angry and sorely deceived man could fling it,—and it was largely made up of a heavy cabbage.

A Violent Remedy.

Bessie sat down rather hard in the middle of the stage and gazed at the crowded and noisy house in amazement, and at Austin in particular, with—

" Oh, Adolphus!—how could you be so rude!" and then there were roars of laughter.

On the card Austin had written hastily, the lines from Byron,

> " I only know we loved in vain,
> I only feel,—Farewell! Farewell!"
> —ADOLPHUS.

At the dinner they gave Austin, to soothe his wounded vanity and to laugh the thing over with fizz, Austin said seriously, " I am cured of ever wanting to speak to another girl as long as I live;—boys, you've done the trick. Henceforth I 'm a misogynist!"

But the very next summer vacation Adolphus changed his mind.

"CHUMS OVER IN OLD SOUTH."

It was a raw winter's night, and Paige drew the curtains close, and told his father to take the easy chair in the corner by the somewhat chilly comfort of the radiator. His father was up from New York on some mysterious Senior Society errand into which his son, then a Junior, dared not pry, and they were sitting after dinner around the lamp over their cigars, and tiny glasses of Benedictine, a bottle of which delectable liqueur, covered with curious labels, the old grad. had brought up with him as a gift.

A number of fellows dropped into the room, and "Boots" presented them, one by one, to "my father, Colonel Paige," with a proud air, for the old. grad. was a fine looking, gray haired old veteran, with an armless sleeve. "Little Jack" Horner came in and amused the Colonel immensely with the account of how he "pushed his exam. papers all over the block" in mathematics that day, and in the same breath discussed with Barrington what sort of a "push" was out to Miss Gradley's dance the night before;—"Great" contending that the Gradleys were "smooth people." And Aldrich moaned because he feared he'd "pinched" a condition in logic, and Little Jack told him to "jolly" Prof. Harker more. And they talked of "digs" and "greasy grinds" and Dwight Hall heelers, and the new style "long cheer," and what a "daisy peach" they saw crossing Chapel Street as they came over to the room, and Paige said it was time to "horse to likker," (referring to the Benedictine) and advised Little Jack not to monkey with the townies down on Church Street or the muckers would "push in his little mug until they bent his back teeth in a scrap with them." All this jargon the old grad. listened to with a most mystified and indulgent expression, and his son felt called upon to translate,—but did n't.

Little Jack looked at the armless sleeve a moment, curiously.

"I wish we'd been in Yale during the war," he said. "I understand whole classes enlisted, —that the students drilled every day on the campus, and that you lost more men after Bull

Run and Shiloh and Antietam than we did after freshman annual."

"Yale did her part in the war," said Colonel Paige. " And there should be a Memorial Hall built to our dead heroes,—as there is at Cambridge."

" I 'll be one of ten thousand to subscribe one dollar," said Little Jack. " It's all the mon I own at present."

"Father could tell you a story," said Boots, looking at his governor, questioningly.

" A story! A war story!" cried Little Jack, eagerly. " Let us have it Colonel.—"

"Oh,—nonsense. I must be going in a minute," said the Colonel, looking at his watch.

" Father,—I wish they could hear it," urged Paige.

"Oh,—I—it's too soon after dinner, my boy."

And the Colonel puffed out a huge ring of smoke.

" See here, Colonel Paige—"and Horner drew his fat little body up to his full height before him. "Do you think you are going to escape from this room,—with an untold tale concealed about your person?"

"How dare you bulldoze an entire stranger this way!" laughed the Colonel, with a most amiable smile.

"Ah,—but you're not an *entire* stranger," said Little Jack quickly, looking at the armless sleeve.

The Colonel laughed. Then he said, out of nothing, "With all your queer lingo,—and your most amazing slang ever invented on the face of the earth,—I don't see,—but what,—but what you are just counterparts of the boys back in the '60s. Mr. Barrington, you would do very well for Jim Haywood,—we were chums over in old South."

"There,—go on, Governor!" exclaimed Paige, eagerly.

"Just let your side whiskers come out, and your hair grow long as your foot-ball eleven does, and wear doe cloth, and cloth gaiters and long boots, and you will do for Jim. Fashions change. Yale boys are about the same, I guess, after all."

"Go on,—Jim Haywood,—father," urged Boots.

There was a little pause and the Colonel, eyeing his son laughingly, began:

"Well, if you boys want it, here goes. As I said, Jim Haywood was my chum over in South. "Old South" is gone now in more senses than one, so is poor Jim. He was a southerner from Savannah. When the war broke out he left college, and was present at the firing on Fort Sumter.

"He joined Lee's army in Virginia and I was in McClellan's second corps in the Peninsula. (Looks at his watch.) Suffice it to say that in '62, in July, after the battle of Gaines Mill, I volunteered for scout duty along the Chickahominy, and so reported to General Hancock, in person.

"We called ourselves scouts, but as we did not do our work in uniform we were practically spies. You see, I got tired of camp life and volunteered to this extra duty for the fun of it, and for a few months I enjoyed enough excitement to last me a lifetime."

A number of fellows dropped in. Little Jack bade them to be quiet, be seated and listen, and the Colonel continued.

"One dark, misty night in August, '62, I was trying to pass the picket line the Johnnies had stretched along from Bethesda Church, over by

McGee's house, in so'eastern Virginia, you know, in the valley of the Chickahominy. I was returning from a three weeks' sojourn in rebel lines, and had several maps sewed in my boots, and some important memoranda. I was in my peddler's disguise,—carried a pack and wore a gray coat, and meal-bag trousers, and slouch hat, and was armed with a 'lead stick,' and had 'iron in my boot,' as they say; that is one revolver, and a loaded cane."

" I got through the rebel lines without much difficulty by dodging the pickets, and made my way along, cross lots, with the aid of a pocket compass, under the glass of which I pressed a firefly; I was beginning to lose that nervous, dreadful feeling I always had when crossing the lines, and was congratulating myself on getting through to the Union Army before daylight. I used to hate daylight! (And right here let me advise any of you lads, if you want real honest excitement, study to be professional burglars, I've often thought of it!) I used to have to hide in hay-mows, or in old barns, or in the swampy woods all day, and the mosquitoes were——you have no idea! But at night I could find my way anywhere. I was young and loved the excitement then, and stood to lose my life twenty times a day without once losing my nerve.

"I was making my way through a piece of swamp and I heard suddenly the word, *Halt!* and a report and blinding flash of fire followed. Luckily I was not hit. I quickly threw myself behind a stump and sank in the mire of a deep pool, and there I waited. I think it was half an hour I sat in water up to my waist in suspense; then I slowly rose out of my hole and looked about me. It was too pitch dark to see ahead ten feet,—but I did n't mind the darkness. I did mind what I heard,—voices in low tones not a dozen yards from me! I knew the Johnnies were searching for me. Presently they lit a lantern, four of them. I could have killed two, possibly, but I did n't know how many more were hid behind the trees, and I thought best, like Brer Fox, to lie low and wait.

"Then after a while, I groped my way, flanking the party to the east, and got to the edge of the open wood, and then it was all up with me. A party of at least fifty Johnnies were camping around a fire and I almost ran in upon them!

"I hid myself as best I could under the thick

bush. Had I come in the wrong direction? Afterwards I discovered that the little contemptible firefly had caught the needle in his left wing and I had in consequence gone west nor'west instead of northeast. I was in the midst of the enemy!

"I skirted the wood as carefully as I could, and then two of the Johnnies hidden behind trees jumped up and seized me. At first I pretended to go along with them and then suddenly knocked one of them down and made a break for the wood,—but the other fellow gave the alarm, fired his gun, and I was captured."

"I told my story,—a yarn I had invented and worked a dozen times. I was a peddler going to Harper's Ferry, to procure some cloth and tobacco for soldiers' use. I had printed newspapers with my ad. in it which I showed them—I was a Jew haberdasher at Harper's Ferry. 'Isaac Helberstein'; but my story did n't seem to take.

"I was disarmed and searched and hurried to camp. I knew the jig was up when they ripped up my boots and found a map of some rebel fortifications around old Cold Harbor in them.

"I was sent with a detail to General L—'s headquarters, and, after a drumhead court-martial was ordered to be shot the following day but one, at sunrise. Then I was remanded to the care of the Captain of the Company who captured me, for execution, and a double guard was set over me in the guard-house.

"'The jig is up,' I said to myself all the next day, 'and all because of a firefly!' The Johnnies pitied me and gave me tobacco and some whisky, and tried to make my last day agreeable; and, as I was pretty weary, I enjoyed it very well. Let me say that a man who is in health, can never really believe he's actually going to die; I'm certain *I* did n't, that twenty-third day of August, 1862. I laughed and joked, and made the Johnnies believe that the war would n't last three months. Death did n't seem so extraordinary in those days of carnage and destruction. I did n't feel it really near me. I wrote a dozen letters to my mother, to my sisters, and to my sweetheart,—his mother,—(looking at Paige with affection). I wrote to old Prex Woolsey and dear Professor Thacher, detailing the facts of my capture,—hard to be shot as a spy, you know, and not have a chance to explain,—and yet I thought of Nathan Hale, too, and I did n't grieve, or complain. It was the chances of war, and war makes a new atmosphere, and we get used to it once we are in it, and don't mind—and if death comes, it comes so lightly and easily that it is hardly sad or a calamity.

"The night passed. I thought of my life at college, my old friends I 'd never see again— but still it was n't so mournful as you 'd think. I wondered what had become of my old chum, Jim Haywood,—I thought of several, too, who had been killed,—I was sure I 'd see *them*. You see, dying in war times in such a glorious company of the heroic dead, is quite a different thing from dying now in peace. I told the Johnnies I was a Yale man. One of them was from a Virginia university, and we became quite friendly. They asked me many questions about college life,—about the Wooden Spoon and the "Bully," and the secret societies. It got noised abroad all over the rebel camp that a Yale man was going to be shot as a spy,—and as you will see, my acknowledging allegiance to dear old mother Yale, thus, saved my life.

"The night passed in comfortable sleep, and dreams of home. I awoke at dawn and felt refreshed. I looked out at the glorious sunrise—was it to be my last? The morning began to get bright. Presently they led me out to the edge of a wood in a little field. A chaplain prayed with me,—I wish I could see that good man again, for his prayer did me lots of good,—it was so long that,—but I must n't anticipate.

"They blindfolded my eyes, and asked me if I was ready. I said 'No, a man is never ready to die!' and some one whispered, 'Dick Paige, at the volley fall forward on your face!

"'How am I to know which side I'll fall on, you fool?' I asked sharply. It was serious business for me just then, and I thought some Johnnie was laughing at me.

"'You fall on your face!—Don't you remember Jim? We were chums away over in old South. *I'm here*, and am officer in charge.'"

"Then he went aside, and I understood.

"My heart stood still with a certain absolute belief that Jim Haywood,—my old chum over in South was going to save my life in some way. Hope sprang up again. I knew Jim. He was one of the cutest fellows that ever lived. I knew that if any one could interfere between those six murderous bullets and my heart,—*he* could. As I stood there, hands tied behind my back, eyes blindfolded,—seeing the red through the handkerchief, the red of the hot, rising sun,—I was as sure I was in a sort of farce play as I was when he and I, as Freshmen, were initiated into old Alpha Sigma Phi,—They trained blank cartridges on us there in college, —everything went to gun-play in those war times, you know; I just trusted Jim, and when they asked me if I cared to say anything, I was just mean enough to seize my advantage and let them have a good, stiff, stump speech on the wickedness of secession, and then I gave them a great bluff about the war's being over in three months and warning them to come in out of the rain. They must have thought me rather cheeky!

"Well, I finished, and listened to Scripture and the last prayer of the chaplain, and was told to prepare for death. I said I was ready, and then came Jim's sharp command: '*Present ar-rums! Make ready ar-rums!*' Then the words in a lower tone,—but I could hear them distinctly in the silence—'Aim at his breast, Johnson. All aim at the breast of the poor devil—there,—ready,—*fire!*'

"I fell forward quickly on my face, and lay still. Was Jim Haywood there? Thank God! *Yes*,—he was, because I was still alive! I lay as if dead, and felt a blanket thrown over me. In some way Jim had drawn those bullets, and prevented the surgeon making any examination.

"Then, after a little, they rolled me in the blanket and carried me away into the woods.

"Then, in my sensitive ear, I heard Jim's voice again: 'We are to bury you, Dick, under a foot of earth. I'll put a musket barrel down to your mouth, don't fret.'

"Then they rolled me into my grave and I felt the earth falling over me, and all was very dark and dismal, I can tell you! I was nearly suffocated before Jim got his tube so as it would work. I suppose he had to be very wary of the guard; but at last he got it in place, and what's more, later on, poured some very comforting whisky into my mouth, which nearly strangled me at first, because I was n't expecting it. But it was grateful, I can tell you. One of the most blessed drinks I ever took in my life, because, lying in my grave that way, so cold, so dark, so immovable,—the fear began to steal over me that perhaps I was really dead, after all! Perhaps I had only been dreaming that my old chum Jim Haywood had whispered to me, and they had buried me, and this *was* death! I no sooner got out of that worry than I began to think I'd been buried alive on purpose,—some fiendish plan to torture my life out by slow degrees. Were you ever buried?"

The Colonel turned to one or two fellows in the room, who laughed.

"Well, it's unutterably horrible, that's all I can say. Creeping, slimy worms crawl over your face, and try to burrow under your eyelids, and ugh! into your ears. You can't move. I imagined they were writhing and creeping into my very brain. I thought I should shriek with the horror of it as that awful day went on;—then, thank God, came the whisky, and I got my head loose in the earth so I could twist it. I could n't hear a sound except the tread of feet on the ground—feet going and coming endlessly. The boom-boom rumble of a heavy gun-carriage,—the cannonading of horses' feet,—the march of infantry,—the light footsteps of some one running. Oh, what a dreadful day that was! and I lay stark and stiff, biting the end of a musket barrel for breath!

"Over and again through my head, I remember, ran the verses in *Maud*,—we knew Tennyson's *Maud* by heart when I was in college, and swore by it:

> ' Dead, long dead. Long dead!
>   And my heart is a handful of dust,
> And the wheels go over my head
>   And my bones are shaken with pain,
> For into a hollow grave they are thrust!'

"Then in the afternoon I grew very tired and weary, and it seemed as if I could feel the swing of the earth as it rolled in space, and I felt myself getting lighter and lighter and rising in the air; and it seemed as if I hung a distance above my grave, and looking down saw the soldiers marching past. Then Jim must have got some whisky down the tube, for I felt myself drawn down to earth again, and amid unutterable pain and anguish I re-entered my body,—and lived.

"Of the two experiences, dying is not half

so hard to endure as coming back to consciousness and taking up again the thread of life,— Nothing has so clearly demonstrated to my mind the presence of a soul in the body, a tenant outside of brain, tissue, flesh, and blood, who at death is released and escapes. I say that is the *conscious* feeling. I also felt great expansion,—freedom, and coming back to my body, and its trivial life seemed narrowing and belittling to me.

"That night Jim and his faithful negro servant, whom I afterwards got installed in South as a sweep,—do any of you remember Alston? —dug me up, resurrected me, and revived me with food and whisky. I lay an hour on the ground sick and faint and unable to move, holding Jim's hand, while he whispered about old times on the fence and on the campus, and tried to cheer me up and get me on my feet. I had a long way to walk that night, as you may believe.

"'Why, old boy! it was not half so bad as the Freshman initiation into Alpha Sigma Phi,' said Jim; 'and don't you remember the Freshman we buried in the campus, and Professor Brown caught us?'

"'I'd rather be shot again than buried again,' I said feebly. 'A bullet is more merciful than a grave.'

"I lay down on the ground behind a tree, while Alston and Jim went to work filling up the grave again. While they were at it, we heard the clattering of horses' hoofs and an officer rode up.

"'What are you doing in that hole?' he asked in a thick, drunken voice. 'Has any one (hic) been body-snatching round yere?'

"'No, Major,' said Jim. 'We received orders to re-examine the clothes of the spy who was shot this morning, and search for further despatches, that's all.'

"The Major leapt off his horse. 'Curse the d——d Yankee spy!' he growled, drawing his sword, and stabbing in the loose earth to the hilt, where I had lain. Somehow, the blade slipping through the miry earth seemed to me to be slipping through my very body also, and I closed my eyes in horror, and faintness.

"The Major wiped his blade with some leaves. 'Curse the d——d Yankee!' he said. 'The Federals in some way have got news of our movements and they have changed their lines.'

"'Well, there is an end of *this* fellow!' said Jim, as Alston filled up the grave and made it even with the surface.

"After some further parley, the Major finally took himself off, and when all was quiet again, I got up and brushed the dirt from my hair and clothes. I could scarcely stand, and Jim Haywood gave me a long pull from his canteen and some scraps of bread and meat, and then we moved off into the woods, and walked along in silence for an hour.

"'I want you to give me your parole you will go home and leave the army when you get back inside the Federal lines,' said Jim, at last.

"'I can't, Jim; I can't leave the army until my time is up.'

"'You *must* give your parole, Dick! It is only fair to me. You are my prisoner, and either you give me your word that you will leave the Federal army, or I'll march you back to camp, and report a capture. You will be sent to Andersonville as a prisoner of war,—we won't shoot you as a spy. But I can't let you go back to your lines and fight against us again. I have more sense of honor than that. That would be aiding and abetting the enemy and not merely saving the life of a friend.'

"'I'll give you my word, Jim, I'll never do any more scouting. I've done with that!'

"'No, that's not enough. I counted on your giving me your parole, Dick. It is only right.'

"'I'll agree to get transferred to the western frontier!'

"'No, give me your word you'll go home, or I'll march you back to camp, where I'll see to it that you are sent a prisoner of war to Andersonville. I won't let them shoot you as a spy, Dick!'

"'Thanks, Jim. You are very kind,' I said. 'But I'm in the fight to stay!'

"Then we sat down side by side on the edge of a cornfield and argued the matter for half an hour. Neither of us liked to give in then any more than we did when we were 'Brothers'* together at Yale. At last Jim got up and said sternly:

"'There is another way to settle this thing.

---

* The Colonel referred to one of the two famous debating societies at Yale, "Brothers" and "Linonia," which ceased to exist in 1873.

If you won't do what is right in one way,—you shall in another. I won't shoot an unarmed man, here, take this pistol. I will advance twenty paces and then turn and we will both commence firing. Whoever survives,—Alston will lead safely to his lines. So! On these terms I release you!'

"'Jim!' I cried, as he handed me a revolver. 'Do you think I can try to kill the man who has just saved my life? Here, shoot me if you like,—I cannot and will not fire at you?'

"He hesitated a moment, wavering; then said, in a harsh voice, I remember, 'You have my final terms!' Then he advanced, counting off his ten paces in the open field. The feeble moonlight trickled down through the fine pine branches of the wood. It was warm and clear. Far off I could hear the roll of the drums. We could not be far from the Federal lines. I felt like making a dash for liberty, but I was too weak and exhausted with that long day's suffocation under ground to attempt it. Besides, I knew that to Jim's sense of Southern chivalry, such conduct would seem all the more cowardly as he had stated the terms of my release, and I was in honor bound to them.

So, you see, I just stood there pistol in hand, looking at Jim.

"He reached his twenty yards, stood a moment his back to me. Alston withdrew behind a pine, out of danger.

"'Make ready, Dick!' called out Jim. 'I'm going to shoot!'

"'God forgive you!' I called back to him, and almost immediately he turned and fired. The first ball flew over my head. The second grazed my shoulder. I looked steadily at Jim, he was firing blindly, his hand over his eyes."

"He fired again! and I felt a sharp sting in my left arm.

"'For God's sake! shoot at *me*, Dick!' he cried, in an agonized voice. But of course I refused. In another instant twenty or thirty men seemed to leap out of the ground and surround us. They were Union soldiers,—the 4th of Ohio,—and my life was saved the third time that day.

"Jim made a show of fight, but was captured and we were all taken to headquarters at once.

"To make a long story short, I represented to General Hancock that Jim had saved my life, and, after a day or two, through my intercession he was discharged and allowed to return to his regiment.

"I never could bring myself to speak to him again. I was sorely wounded in the arm and in the hospital—I could not forgive him then and requested not to see him when he was released. Poor Jim Haywood was killed in the Wilderness before Richmond. Later on, I have come to regard his conduct with less feeling of anger and astonishment, and with more charity. In his Southern nature and education, he had only done what he believed to be the honorable thing to his cause and to his friend.

"The result of his third shot,—combined with a surgeon's bungling—principally the latter—I carry with me to this day—" and amid a breathless silence the Colonel lifted the stump of his arm and let it fall.

"All I can add is that I owe my life to my dear old Alma Mater—and to Jim—my old chum over in South—Boys, War is a cursed sort of thing—and a war between friends is—awful!"

Then Colonel Paige, visibly affected, rose, buttoned up his coat, was helped on with his overcoat and hat, and shaking hands with a number of Boots' friends,—left the room.

COMMENCEMENT.

> " Some back from the threshold shrink,
>   As loath from the past to part,
> But the most plunge over the brink
>   With never a fear at heart."

> " Then silent closes the door
>   At the sound of the last old chime,
> And the key,—for evermore,
>   Is turned by the keeper, Time !"
>
> SCOLLARD.

BEFORE the day of large classes, Commencement * (so-called because it comes at the *close* of the college year) formerly ended the four years of student life at Yale in a glory of scholastic furor and excitement. It was a sort of annual parade of the learning and scholarship of every member of the class. Fifty and a hundred years ago our forefathers debated in set Latin phrases,

---

* This year (1895) marks a great change in the Yale Commencement exercises. Many improvements in the speaking have been made. Music is now a greater feature of the programme. Commencement is now to be made a *pleasurable* occasion.

held dialogues in Greek, and established tremendous reputations for learning, among the open eyed and astonished audience of mothers, sisters, cousins, and aunts who, through the long, hot Commencement Day, heard of and marvelled at the heroes of Greece and Rome and the various dignitaries of the ancient world, and all the virtues and defects of the pagans, with hardly an allusion to the stirring life about them.

Among many of the smaller rural colleges the custom is still maintained of making Commencement Day an annual exhibit of students and faculty. The latter sit in solemn state upon the stage. One by one, in all the garish light of day, appear the pale and terrified Seniors, in evening dress, and make their parting bow. It means something to graduate when one may be overwhelmned by bouquets and see one's relations in tears over an eloquent peroration upon the " Age of Pericles." There is a keen excitement in seeing one's younger brother, at home a modest, amusing, and unassuming young fellow enough, suddenly displayed before an audience as a defender of Oliver Cromwell, or a patron of Washington. At Yale it comes to but few to display their gifts of oratory. All of our heroes, excepting the good Deacon Demarest and Averill, received their degree in batches of eight or ten and in silence or amid the warbling of a brass band. Once they received their "sheep-skins," they rushed out on the green in boisterous squads and fought and tussled for the precious labels of scholarship—the very A.B.'s of the real life to come!

Commencement came to them with a curious mingling of humor and sentiment,—bringing a realizing sense of desolate partings, and the packing of dusty books; of farewells, and bargaining off of old furniture to fresh young gentlemen of rosy cheeks and hopeful tendencies; of teas and dances and jollity, and dismal preparations to leave the old place forever.

It seemed quite absurd to them to see their familiar classmates fluttering and fussing about among the "queens" in their unfamiliar black Oxford gowns, and mortar boards,—it gave them all a weird, uncanny look, as Miss Kitty Nelson oftimes remarked. Little Jack called the black gowns shrouds, and went about in his, looking utterly ridiculous, but sad and disconsolate, and spoke in lowered tones, as if at a funeral.

The proverbial Commencement weather, of course, was "hot, hotter, hottentottest," and the Senior Prom, Glee Club concert, and Harvard ball game, and Class Histories were enjoyed in a state of pleasing and warm appreciation, which did all the greater credit to their remarkable class.

A great crowd turned out on the Campus to listen to "Little Jack's" history, and it was sufficiently veracious to be embodied in this bundle of stories without any alteration. Among other matters, he told of the bonfires which the class had built, in spite of the faculty, in Soph. year.

"In the spring term of Soph. year," he said, "the faculty issued a decree that there should be no more bonfires started on the Campus in celebration of athletic victories. They were afraid of injuring the grass [*Laughter*]; but we, who had studied phleebottomy of the class of Umpty Three,—knew that a bonfire was useful in destroying the worms on the elm leaves, and decided to have one.

"The ingenious plan was suggested by no other than good "Deacon" Demarest [*Laughter*]. A hundred men were each to secretly provide themselves with a box or a barrel, filled with hay and saturated with kerosene. And then, as the chapel bell struck nine o'clock, each holder of barrel or box was to run at top speed to a certain spot, deposit his *lignum flammæ*, and hurry away again into outer darkness, unrecognized by friend or foe.

"This was done as the chapel bell tolled out the hour, that night—From out the darkness, flying to a common centre, as if by witchcraft, came the hundred boxes and barrels, and soon a noble pile was the result. The last man lit the pile, and a sheet of flame roared heavenward, which drove the worms into their holes forever—a flame which the faculty could not approach and molest, so fervent was the heat—and around which we danced until the morn, and celebrated our victorious team.

"Then the faculty posted a second edict, that no bonfires should be *built* in the College yard, and any one found building such a fire, should be forthwith expelled!

"But a Princeton victory occurred the next week, and the good Deacon was quite equal to the emergency. An old disused farm wagon was purchased from a blacksmith, and under cover of night was loaded with most excellent tar barrels,—yea, verily, the load of tar barrels reached the height of some twenty cubits on the wagon.

"Then a modest but stalwart band of Dwight Hall heelers drew the wagon to the Elm Street entrance on the Campus, and some ingenious deacon touched the affair off with a lighted match. [*Laughter.*]

"Then, as quietly as possible, they ran the wagon in on the Campus and tried to knock off a wheel, so that it should not thereafter be removed by meddling members of the faculty, but there was no time for this—and the heelers had to fly to their rooms, and leave the wagon to its fate.

"The fire got well going; the blaze promptly reached the elm branches and destroyed what worms were left. Then the fun began. You see,—it wasn't *started* on the Campus. And when the faculty came out in full force they could accuse no one, and the tutors and monitors tried to drag the wagon out of the yard. It was quite as warm near that wagon as it is here to-day, and they 'd try to drag it a little way, and then have to beat a retreat in a half scorched condition. It was the hottest fire I, or any other member of the faculty, ever saw. I assure you it makes the temperature rise ten degrees about me here, to read this yarn—but the truth of history must prevail! [*Laughter.*]

"They got a long rope and dragged the affair across the yard behind the buildings, toward the Art School; then they found that the coppers would n't let them carry it out into Chapel Street, and they turned it around and toted it along towards Alumni Hall. Then a lot of students got hold of the rope and they ran the bonfire down to Durfee, and then Professor Dribble came out and got very angry indeed, and ordered it pulled over to the Library and out into High Street. So over there it went,—a wonder it did n't set every dormitory on the Campus afire!—And when last seen, it was blazing away in the old gym. lot."

"Well, the faculty gathered in a lot of names,—but the testimony all went to show that the fire was not *built* on the Campus, and so no one of the Dwight Hall heelers was ever punished. [*Laughter.*] They changed the wording of the edict next day, and it now reads, 'Anyone who shall assist in building a bonfire on the Campus, or bring such fire upon the Campus, shall be expelled.' But I expect that in some way obscure to us now, future students will manage to evade this just, yet terrible law."

The ".Crowd" played a final joke on Little Jack himself, as he finished his history and bowed amid the applause of the surrounding open-air amphitheatre. As the fat little chap stood bowing and smiling upon the platform, a bouquet was thrown to him, and, as he blushed and stooped to pick it up, it crept along the stage; he stooped for it,—and it vanished, amid great laughter! One of the Crowd, whom he'd been guying more or less unmercifully, had tied a fish line to the bouquet with a nefarious design to get even. But Little Jack merely laughed and said of the bouquet, "Not lost, but gone before," and was more popular than ever.

They helped plant the class ivy on the Library wall; they chanted the Ivy Ode, a graceful effort of Barrington's; they took in the Art Reception, and danced for the last time with some of the pretty girls, but they left early, voting it a rather melancholy affair.

They attended the spread in Alumni Hall. They bade farewell to everybody and everything; then they gathered on the fence in front of Durfee, with Little Jack in their midst and there was a silent smoke together. The last smoke as undergrads.

"Do you remember," said Barrington, after a long silence, "when we roomed up on York Street, Paige, how the name 'Boots' got fitted onto you? The Sophs. broke into our room and made you and me stand on chairs and recite hymns, and the only hymn you could think of was:

> 'I hear those boots, those b-b-b-boots
> A coming down the stairs,
> Fra Diavolo,—the Robber!
> Fra Diavolo,—the opera!'

"We all took it up as a class song afterward, and a good one it is, too. Oh, those Freshman days! It seems a long while ago, now, does n't it? I wish we had them to live over again. I'm sure we'd be better, work harder, see the advantages of study!"

"Rats!" said several. "We've done very well as it is. We've not been dropped."

"I would n't care, if we were all going to be together somewhere," said Little Jack, mournfully.

"We'll all go up to New London."

"And then?"

"Oh, the world's yawning for us."

"Yes, if it's half asleep it is!" said Little Jack. "But I don't think the world intends to be caught napping!"

How silent and dark the buildings looked! Most of them seemed to have already donned their vacation habiliments of woe. Lights glimmered from but few windows, and these presumably of some weary tutor pursuing the evanescent and illusive "average" through a mass of Sophomoric examination papers.

The moonlight trickled down through the elm branches on the turrets and towers of the old library and the mass of dormitory and old chapel steeple,—its mystic influence concealed the defects, the architectural blemishes of the rugged brick lines, and made an idealization possible of the Yale that was now lost to them forever.

The Campus, with the white tent in front of Alumni Hall, where the swarm of grads. had encamped, was now invaded by a horde of dusky savages, baggage wagons, and a sound of rattling plates. To add to the mournfulness of the scene, a dog shut up in some upper room in Farnam, made night hideous with his agonizing howls.

"That's Elmer's dog 'Pat,'" said Paige. "He's gone out to a reception, I suppose, and locked Pat in his room."

Little Jack said nervously, "I hope Elmer is coming back soon." He edged himself up on the fence.

"Do you remember the small white bull-terrier I had when I roomed with old Waters, in South Middle, Soph. year? Do you remember Fannie? I got her third term Freshman. She was a thoroughbred! Somehow, hearing that dog, I keep thinking of poor little Fannie, the only creature I think I ever really loved. She lies buried here in the Campus.

"She could do no end of tricks, brought me my pipe, my slippers, could dance on her hind legs. I thought the world of her, little beauty! She would hear my whistle and run to me wherever I was. How well I remember her short, sharp little bark! She fell sick and I fed her her meals from a teaspoon. She would n't let any one else feed her. I watched over her and nursed her to life again. She had a little way of sitting up at my window on the fourth story in South, and watching for me. Poor little Fan!

"'Sport'" Waters was fond of her, too, in his way,—she was a first-class ratter, and we had some fun with her in the room. When she got her dander up, she was n't afraid of anything in the world! She knew as much as a human being, too; she saved my life once, waking up and barking when the student lamp got afire, and my bed caught and would have burned me alive. Waters was out and I fell asleep, reading in bed. Well,—you can believe I thought a good deal of Fannie after that!

"She was with us at New London, when I was cox on the crew, and she had as sharp an eye for good rowing, as any man I ever saw. Sometimes they 'd let me carry her in the boat. Oh, every-one in New London knew Fannie that year!

"Well, one warm night in October it was,— Sport and I were going over to dinner, and we were in a hurry and came away from the room, and snapped the door to and left Fannie shut up inside, by accident. When we got down in the yard, we thought of her, but I was too d——d lazy to go back up four flights for her and let her out.

"I looked up at the window,—and, by Jove! it had been carelessly left open, and there stood Fan, looking down and barking,—her dear little head on one side, in the way she had.

"Well,—I think Waters unthinkingly whistled to her, she saw us, and, good God! she gave a little whine and jumped! We were hurrying away,—and you know a dog,—we did n't see her; all we heard was a dull thud,—and there lay poor Fannie, perfectly still on the stone side-walk. I picked her up gently; she was not quite dead, her back broken, though. I carried her upstairs. I did n't want any dinner that night. I went up to the room and laid her down on the sofa, and I confess, I cried! Oh, I was a boy then, you know!—I put my arms around her, and, just feebly trying to lick my hand with her tongue,—she died,"

"That's a nice yarn to tell to-night!" said Aldrich, gloomily.

But Little Jack continued:

"When Sport Waters came in from dinner, he looked at Fannie,—and then, without a word, he went right out and got on a jag. It was his way, poor Waters, to drown his feelings. He got full the day he was dropped, too.

"That night we went out and got a spade, and we secretly buried Fannie, half a dozen of us, at the foot of an elm. Dear little dog!"

There was a short silence.

"And I feel fellows, that that's the way I'm always going to be out in the cold world—too d——d selfish and lazy and careless all my life. I could n't even go up and get Fannie,—and I'm blue as indigo, and,—and,—I wish I was just coming down from Andover, instead of being on the outside now,—and—and——"

Paige put his arms around Little Jack's neck and hugged him.

"Great" Barrington said, sharply:

"Boys,—it's too d——n dismal out here! I'm going over to the Club for a little 'lemonade.' Will you all come along?"

And they all followed him, for the last time.

THE END.

www.ingramcontent.com/pod-product-compliance
Lightning Source LLC
Chambersburg PA
CBHW030729230426
43667CB00007B/652